TAKE MY LIFE

Philippa Shelley is a young opera singer who, on the night of her first successful appearance at Covent Garden, sees her husband, Nicolas Talbot, in close conversation with a girl violinist who has been playing in the orchestra. She discovers that the girl, Elizabeth Rusman, is a former mistress of his who is intent on renewing their acquaintance, and this leads to a violent quarrel between Philippa and her husband, during which Nick receives a wound on his head and rushes out angrily into the night.

Philippa, now all remorse, awaits Nick's return, but he does not come. Instead, early in the morning, she is visited by two police officers who tell her that her husband has been detained for questioning in connection with the murder of Elizabeth Rusman.

With horror she discovers that a great weight of circumstantial evidence is building up against Nick, and that the police are sure they have caught their man. She alone is certain that he is innocent, and she sets out to prove it, an enterprise which, as she gets nearer and nearer the truth, leads her into acute danger herself.

When this story was filmed a distinguished critic said of it that it 'introduces the stir of violence into the world of ordinary people and so has the chill of real horror, because it might have happened to you or me'.

Take My Life

WINSTON GRAHAM

THE BODLEY HEAD
LONDON   SYDNEY
TORONTO

All rights reserved
ISBN 0 370 00594 5
Printed in Great Britain for
The Bodley Head Ltd
9 Bow Street, London, WC2E 7AL
by Redwood Burn Limited
Trowbridge & Esher
Set in Monotype Garamond
First published 1947
This edition 1965
Fourth impression 1976

For Valerie Taylor
who first suggested it and
who worked with me throughout
on the original screenplay –
in affection and esteem

Chapter One

A YEAR OR SO after the end of the war an Italian opera company visited London.

There in the loveliest theatre in England, under the gold insignia of the young queen (Victoria), and surrounded (at a distance) by the faded lettuce leaves, horse droppings, flower petals, bits of blown straw and stray tomatoes of the district's other industry, they gave a season of the familiar works of Rossini, Verdi, Puccini and Leoncavallo.

Certain features distinguished this company from others which had come and gone before; its enthusiasm, its unevenness of performance, its occasional extravagances and occasional brilliances, and its lack of elderly overweight prima donnas. There was also the phenomenon that among its principal sopranos it included an English girl.

Philippa Shelley had been studying at Milan in 1939. Desperately wanting to finish her course under Ruggero, she had stayed on during the 'phoney' war, and then, with Europe crumbling about her, she had timed her exit twenty-four hours late and had paid for her error with four years' internment in Sicily.

Soon after her release she had come in contact with the two high officers, one British and one American, who had sponsored an operatic venture for the entertainment of their troops, and within a month she had been singing *La Bohème* in Palermo. As all southern Italy fell into the net of the Allies, so the talent on which they could draw became wider, and at Naples and later in Rome Philippa had sung with all the leading Italians of the day. At the end of the war she had returned to England for a short time, but, finding no immediate opportunities, had made her way to France and then back to Italy. She had been very quickly offered an appointment by the directors of the San Giovanni Opera Company of Rome, who even after twelve months still occasionally paused to wonder at this strange fair northern girl who had not only been trained in Italy but in some curious manner had imbibed the ability to sing as usually only Italians could sing, born and bred to the hot sun and the smell of grape vines, people with free-flowing Latin temperaments to whom singing was an inherent gift and these songs familiar since childhood.

Sometimes she seemed, unfairly, to have other qualities which many of their own singers lacked, acting ability, dramatic intelligence, a consistent quality of being able to live the part so that there was a rare emotional fusion of song and story. The directors of the San Giovanni had a very good idea of her general talents and would by now have angled her into signing a long-term contract at a relatively low salary if it had not been for the disagreeable influence of her husband, the British officer.

Seventeen minutes before the curtain was due to rise on the first night at Covent Garden the Disagreeable Influence was picking his way among the back-stage commotion in the direction of his wife's dressing-room. Nicolas James Talbot, M.C., late Captain in the Coldstream Guards, was a well-set, good-looking young man, with a good-tempered easy poise and a charm of manner which generally had the effect of putting other people at their ease. Among the haste and last-minute disorganization of opening night, with final questions and instructions flung in a furious bombardment about his ears, he seemed to be the one calm man, the spectator at a curious battle, the detached observer with nothing to gain or lose. It would have taken a perceptive person to have seen that under the shell of his calm, tensions and anxieties moved freely enough, no less acute for having no visible outlet.

In the dressing-room he found Franco Paroni, the conductor, exchanging confidences with Philippa which would have been better unspoken since they only repeated *da capo* the advice of the last rehearsal and the rehearsal before that. Paroni was always a bundle of nerves before a concert, and excitement is no less infectious back stage than measles in the schoolroom. Nick Talbot edged him conversationally towards the door and through it; then Philippa found an excuse to send her dresser on an errand, and they werè alone.

Even then, for a little while, though she rose at once to kiss him, he was aware of something separating them. It was always the same at these times: the opera star had a firm grip over the girl he had married. He did not mind, for they were both expressions of the one personality that he loved. Gently he listened to her last-minute complaints about the floats, which she said were too bright, to her doubts about the aria in Act Two, to her doubts of the opera itself, *Butterfly*, which he knew she did not like as well as some of the others and which she had come to imagine was not as popular with the British public as it had once been, to her regrets that *Traviata* had not been chosen to begin when Maddaleni, whom she greatly preferred, would have been conducting, and Ronsi singing with her.

On all these things he chidingly reassured her, aware nevertheless that tonight the nervous strain was greater than it had ever been before.

At length she said: 'It's my own people, that's truly what I'm scared of tonight. In Italy I was a stranger, appearing before people of a different race. They may be just as critical – even more so; but that isn't what counts. When I was a little girl and my father and mother were away, I sang a song at a local concert and was a huge success. When they came back they asked me to sing it in my own drawing-room and I was a dismal flop. Well . . . don't you see? This is my own drawing-room. And somehow those people out there will know it. . . .' She shivered. 'Put your arms round me,' she whispered, 'and tell me I'm infallible.'

He did so, and held her tight.

'That's very easy,' he said. 'You are infallible, darling. . . . But maybe that's only for me. As for the others, I'll tell you something you already know, you old fraud. That even when you sing badly you still have something no one else has. Just remember that. It's something no one and nothing can take from you, and we're going to get it to-night as we've never had it before. As for looks, you're far the most beautiful opera singer I've ever seen—'

'Oh, you're prejudiced—'

'Looks count. Perhaps they shouldn't, but they do. And you can act; that's still more rare. You're infallible and you know it. In an hour *they'll* know it. Believe me.'

'I wish you were coming with me,' she said. 'Out there on the stage. I shouldn't mind then.'

'I shall be. As near as I possibly can be in the box. If you want me any time, just whistle and I'll hop out and join you.'

She smiled. He was conscious of something changing in her attitude, as if her muscles were less taut.

'Remember that first night in Naples,' he said. 'You fairly bowled me over. Perfection in a woman. I thought by your eyes you were not Italian, but I never dared to hope you'd be English. Crikey! I went every night that week, and it wasn't until the last night that I dared . . . Remember my humble and nervous approach? Knees fairly knocking. I'd far rather have faced the audience out there. . . .'

He talked on, trying in the few short minutes left to give her ease and confidence. Then Marie, her dresser, came in and got out the dark wig and darted meaning glances at the clock.

Silently Talbot put a hand in his pocket and took out a small crystal elephant. With a side glance at Marie he handed it to Philippa.

The girl looked down at it a moment and then, touched, smiled up into his eyes.

'. . . Every time you've given me one of these they've done the trick.'

'That's what they're for,' he said.

'Remember, Nick, when I get out on the stage I'm going to forget all those white faces and think I'm just singing to you.'

He said: 'Suits me. . . . All right, now?'

She nodded. 'All right.'

He squeezed her arm and went out, began to walk back to his box.

For all his assumed certainties he had moments of doubt as he threaded his way through the theatre-goers moving about the long corridors of the Opera House. He had not the slightest doubt of her capacities, but so much hung on tonight. Tastes, he knew, differed; and what might please an Italian audience would not necessarily please an English one, even though the Italians might be considered the better judges. It was the one danger, and he did not know enough about opera to be as sure as he sounded. And unlike her, he had no real fancy for a continental life. While he was stationed in Italy it had been

11

splendid to be in the same city or within easy train or car distance of each other. Now that he was demobilized it was a different story. Poor at languages, unsympathetic to the Latin, he longed to make England or America their ground. This performance would largely decide their future.

When he reached the box he was met by the harmonious conversation of the orchestra just below him; the tenor squeak of the violins, the reedy baritone of the cellos, upward trips of a flute; one, two, three, like a child climbing a stair. It was all tunefully noisy and warm and exciting.

Joan Newcombe and Leslie had arrived, and he greeted his sister and her son with pleasure. It was the eleven-year-old Leslie's first visit to opera, and he had been allowed to come as a special treat. He was shinier and smoother and neater than Nick had ever seen him before, as if he had been scrubbed and polished with an unsparing hand.

'I say, Uncle Nick,' he began in a stage whisper, 'this is a ringside seat. How did you get it?'

'Influence,' Nick said. 'I know the star slightly. But don't think this is going to be a boxing match. Philippa doesn't fight the conductor or anything. At least we hope not.'

Joan smiled at him. The wine-red taffeta she was wearing brought out all the well-remembered colours in her hair.

'Is she nervous?'

'A bit. But she'll be all right.'

'It's "house full", I suppose?'

'Yes. They're allowing thirty in for standing, but there was a queue of about a hundred when I looked out just now.'

'Uncle Nick,' Leslie said, 'you might tell me when to clap. A fellow at school says it's bad form to make a row in the wrong place.'

Staring over the audience, Nick said: 'I'll sit beside you and pinch you when it's our turn to make a noise.'

They were all in their seats now: that was a blessed regulation about closing the doors.

Tier upon murmuring tier, box upon box, talking and settling, programmes lifted and let fall like leaves in an errant breeze. It was like the inside of a great loaf-shaped wedding cake, like a great inverted wedding cake, with all the icing on the bottom tiers. As your eyes climbed towards the roof, so the luxury and the brilliance exhausted itself in rows of peering anonymous faces staring down at the sugared almonds below. But they, the people in the gallery and the upper circles, were no less arbiters of the night's success than the well-fed critics in the front rows of the stalls.

The critics were numerous tonight, according to the manager. And other distinguished people were present.

The curtain was going to be late; a bad thing, liable to fray a performer's nerves and to make an audience out of patience.

At last a little ripple of clapping spread about the house as Paroni made his appearance. Last-minute fears were gone, and he was master of the situation now. A moment's consultation with his first violin, a rap, rap of his baton; the rustling and movement in the audience faded to a thin hissing murmur; the murmur died and there were a few moments of breathing quiet with a white cloak or a woman's arm luminous in the half shadows of the boxes. Then Paroni raised his baton and the opera began.

Chapter Two

THE WHEEL OF LONDON moved a turn. The earliest congestion of traffic had eased. In the half-lit dark people moved too, singly and in groups, hasty and leisured, strolling and talking, jostled each other, waited to cross, queued for the cinemas, crowded in milk-bars, moved furtively round chemists' shops, argued and elbowed and sneezed and loitered and spat.

Stars had moved up the sky and been obscured by a freckle of rain. A cold breeze beat up the narrower streets, and the bright cheap women of the town – those who had not retired after the war years – moved into convenient doorways and stamped their feet and talked about the influenza. A man in a grey weatherproof turned up the collar of his coat and edged into the stage door of the Opera House. The doorkeeper glanced up from his last edition extra, but seeing that he came no farther and had the look of a gentleman, did not question him.

In the first box on the right Nick Talbot sat rather tautly, keen brown eyes fixed on the stage, nostrils a little flared. From time to time he smiled slightly. Beside him his sister, graceful and bright-eyed but a little languid, sat with one hand on her son's arm.

After half an hour's fascinated gazing at his new aunt, Leslie had begun to taste a few moments of boredom. He had kept it at bay so far by a number of mutely gleeful discoveries about the mechanics of the evening. The hairy hand with the gold signet ring which popped like a spider out of the small box at the front of the stage to turn over the pages of a just visible book, the curious periscope-like thing on which apparently a tiny mirror was set so that Hairy-Hand could see the conductor; the occasional glimpses of stage hands moving in the wings; these gave him something fresh to watch when the business of the evening dragged or he couldn't follow the story.

And there was something very interesting about the great lighted cavern of the orchestra pit, where every kind of musical instrument sawed and boomed and squeaked away; some even hidden under the stage, and all trying to drown poor Aunt Philippa just when she wanted to say something most.

By way of further change he could glance up and about the darkened auditorium with its bright 'EXITS' staring at him like cats' eyes from every turn and tier, but this sooner or later earned him a reproving squeeze from his mother's hand and brought him back to the stage.

An unexpected diversion came when he was the first to notice that a strange man in evening dress had entered their box and was trying to attract Uncle Nick's attention. Leslie nudged the absorbed man beside him, and Talbot turned with an angry frown to know the reason of the interruption. Apologetically the man came a little forward and whispered something about Captain Talbot being wanted on the telephone. There was a brief irritated exchange, and then Nick's frown cleared and with a shrug of apology to Joan Newcombe he crept out of the box.

He was gone some minutes, and by the time he came back the first act was near its end. The curtain came down to a good deal of warm applause, but by the time the actors and actresses came forward to take their bows, some people in the stalls were already pushing their way out towards the bar where a thoughtful management had provided a cold buffet as well as the usual coffee and drinks.

Under his breath Nick cursed the impatient and the ill-mannered, at the same time giving a brief explanation to Joan of his own apparent lapse. He was in fact elated as a result of his telephone call, and when the curtain had fallen for the fifth and final time he took Leslie out into the bar and bought him a drink of ginger pop. There, under the large muscular painting of Ariadne and Bacchus, he sipped whisky and listened to the conversation of the people about him.

It was too early yet; opinions were only just forming. The usual mixed crowd: the imitation beaver and the Burton suit rubbing shoulders with mutation mink and Savile Row.

He hoped Philippa hadn't noticed his going out. It would be so much more fun if he could tell what he had to tell as a surprise and not as an apology.

'Why don't people circulate instead of standing here in this fantastic crush. . . ?'

'My tip for the National is Benny's Joy. An outsider, you know. . . .'

'They say she's English but she *came* from Italy. I wonder if it's a publicity stunt. . . .'

'Yes, pure silk damask, my dear. They're absolute bliss. But I'm terrified they may fade.'

'Are you enjoying it?' – 'Well, I feel I ought to be in a dinner-jacket.'

'She trusts much more to a pure undisturbed cantilena than is usual these days. I think she'll go far.'

'I've been to the counter, but they say I have to buy a ticket somewhere first.'

'The scene struck me as rather tawdry. Did they bring it from Italy. . . ?'

'Yes, it's practically the only place to eat nowadays. . . .'

'So I told her. I said, if she *expected* an *au pair* to do that sort of thing . . .'

'These sentimental operas. If one *thinks* of *Otello* . . .'

'Come on, Leslie,' said Nick. 'There's the first bell, and we'd better be getting back.'

The second act he knew would be the crucial test. Dramatically and musically the finest of the three, it offered all the opportunities of the evening. And within ten minutes of the curtain rise he knew she had 'got' them.

There was a different sort of interest and attention in the audience now. Before it had been a friendly one made up of two thousand separate individuals; now suddenly it had become one big approving beast. Applause broke out after each of the arias, and after the duet with Suzuki, whose lovely little mezzo voice was a perfect foil to Philippa's, it would not be restrained. From then on there was dead silence until the end, where Philippa stood against the blue dawn of the latticed window with her servant sleeping at her feet. The curtain came down in dead silence, and then the applause burst. For a few minutes the lure of the light refreshments was forgotten and the curtain was parted and allowed to fall time after time. Then Philippa was given a curtain to herself and the whole house stood up and roared.

'Uncle Nick,' cried Leslie, trying to make himself heard, 'you've pulled your programme to pieces.'

Nick patted the boy soundlessly on the head and grinned at Joan and thumped the plush rim of the box. The thing he had not expected was that she should be a *greater* success in her own country. Strangely he felt he might start blubbering, which was a curious way of showing his triumph. When at length the interval was fully under way he did not go down into the bar or the foyer but talked in monosyllables to Joan, keeping his fingers crossed and wishing that this was the end of the whole performance. For if the second act of *Butterfly* holds most of the opportunities, the third holds most of the pitfalls, many of them dramatic rather than musical. But there was nothing really to *fear*, except a certain amount of anti-climax, and that could never really affect the judgement of the evening.

At the stage-door a crony had come across from 'The Belvedere' to talk about Pool results with George.

'How's it going?' he said presently, with a jerk of the head towards the interior.

'Oh, they near took the roof off after the second act. Reminds you of the old days. It'll be a quarter of an hour yet before it's done. What I say is, it's always worth 'aving a gamble with one or two entries. It don't cost you no more, and there's the chance . . . Do something for you, sir?'

The stranger in the dark trilby hat hesitated. 'No, thank you. I'm waiting for someone.'

'Best wait outside. There'll be a lot of comin' and goin' through that door soon.'

'When I'm in the way I'll move,' said the man.

The doorkeeper stared coldly at him a moment, and then thought it was not worth exerting his authority – yet. He turned back to his coupons.

Chapter Three

THE CURTAIN HAD been down a dozen times, the clapping, at first explosive, had taken on the character of a bush fire, dying here, spreading there, fanned to fresh flames at each raising of the curtain. It was not the ovation of the second act, but it confirmed and verified Philippa's success beyond all doubt.

Nick got up.

'Come along,' he said, his hands tingling. 'We'll get behind before the corridors fill up.'

As they walked round a number of people were already trickling out, intent on getting the first overcoat or bus or taxi. Some were talking excitedly of the performance, others vacantly, disjointedly, of homely personal things as if the opera had already dropped out of their minds.

They were held up by a press of people at the last door, and Philippa had reached her dressing-room before them.

There were people round her already. She was flushed, still tense, but happy and just beginning to relax. She was trying hard not to believe it, but she knew in her heart she had been the success of the evening. The best had happened. Paroni, who had been on the stage, was here, and a woman reporter had somehow squeezed in, together with a half-dozen notabilities.

Nick found a gap for himself and bent and kissed her. She squeezed two of his fingers.

'Marvellous, darling!'

She nodded. 'I think it's going to be all right, Nick.'

'What do I tell her?' said Paroni, modestly shaking his pince-nez at Nick. 'She follow my beat and she is a star!'

'Miss Shelley,' said the woman reporter, 'it's said that you're Italian-born; is that true?'

'Ruggero taught her,' came a deep voice in the background. 'The technique is unmistakable.'

'My dear Miss Shelley, it's never been sung better. I thought of Marcella Zembrich. And what's more, it's never *looked* better. . . .'

At that moment there was an eruption at the door, and Ravogli, the director of the San Giovanni Theatre in Rome, who had travelled with the company, came in in great style and put his arms round Philippa in a great bear hug.

Joan Newcombe, who had managed to kiss her sister-in-law and murmur words of congratulation, withdrew slowly from the others.

Leslie said: 'I told Aunt Phil I liked that song just before she blindfolded the little boy. I liked the twiddley bits. And that one she sang while you were out, Uncle Nick, that was a good one.'

'I think we should be going, Nick,' his mother said. 'It's been a rare pleasure to me. Such a pity John couldn't be here to see Philippa's triumph.'

'Bring him one night next week,' Nick suggested. 'That's if you can persuade him to face it for the sake of seeing Philippa. They're doing this again next Saturday, and *Traviata* on Wednesday. I'll get you a taxi.'

They left the dressing-room and walked to the stage door. The fine drizzle had changed to a soft gentle rain. He was lucky with a taxi, and in a few minutes he had shut the door on them and with a farewell wave turned in again at the stage entrance.

. . . The orchestra was leaving in ones and twos. Some of the lesser lights of the company also. A number of them glanced at the well-built, brown-eyed man as he walked through them, nodding a friendly good night here and there. He was good to look at, with a distinction of carriage, an unemphasized maleness, which would make him very attractive to women. It had done so in the past. And the past had not quite forgotten him.

As he came near the door of Philippa's dressing-room he passed a girl carrying a violin case. She looked at him casually and then turned.

'Nick!'

He stopped, half turned also, puckered his eyes a little in the badly lit passage. But the truth was that his eyes were trying to reassure him that his ears were wrong.

'Elizabeth!'

She put down her violin case.

'I do believe you were going to cut me dead.'

'I certainly was,' he said. 'Because I didn't see you. I never dreamt of meeting you here!'

She put out one of her hands, and he took it.

'It's a long time, Nick. I've thought about you so often. Have you ever thought about me? No, don't answer! Don't spoil it just now.'

She was a very dark young woman, with fine eyes of a dark amber brilliance; a girl who might look ravishingly pretty sometimes and plain at others. Her mouth had little shadows about it, made by the curl of her bottom lip and the fullness of the contours round it.

'What are you doing here?' he said.

'Playing in the orchestra. And you? Have you been in the army?'

'Yes, five years. In Libya and Italy.'

'How's Spot?' she asked eagerly.

'Dead. The year after.'

'Broken heart?'

He shook his head. 'No. Distemper.'

They both laughed, though not without constraint. Her reappearance was to him like an old song sung out of the past; she belonged to another life, a carefree, feckless, irresponsible, pre-war existence for which, although he had enjoyed it, he had no regrets.

'It's extraordinary our meeting like this,' she said. '*Isn't* it extraordinary? You haven't changed at all. Have I? No, don't tell me that either. I expect I must have in some ways, because all sorts of things have happened to me. I suppose it's been my own fault. But what are you doing here? It's astonishing to meet you back stage.'

He hesitated briefly. 'I'm waiting for my wife.'

She glanced quickly up at him for a second, startled, resentful, then in another second accepting it.

'So you've done it at last. . . .'

'I've done it at last.'

'No wonder you didn't seem very friendly.'

With his old instinct to avoid hurting people he said: 'Of course I'm friendly. I'm tremendously pleased to see you again, and quite honestly you've not changed a bit.'

At once she seized on his reassurance, the sulky lines of her mouth melting away. 'I've a lot to tell you, Nicky. These war years have been a lifetime. I've made rather a mess of things. I'd like to tell you about it. Couldn't we – meet somewhere? It would be fun – and so like old times.'

He smiled a little in spite of himself. It was the same Elizabeth. But he wanted to end the interview. He noticed one or two of the cast glancing curiously at them as they went out.

'You'll be in London some time?'

'I don't know. I'm booked here for at least a week. It was terrific luck getting it, but so many were down with flu.'

'Give me your address,' Nick said. 'Then probably one day later in the week—'

'You wouldn't come. If I gave it you, you wouldn't come. And I'm in such a mess, Nick! I really need advice; sober, sensible advice of the sort you could give.'

Their eyes met again. 'Then I'll come,' he said. 'If I can really be of help to you, I'll come.'

She said: 'It's a miserable neighbourhood. Loften Street. Not far from Euston Road.'

He felt in his pocket and brought out the tattered corner of the programme he had pulled to pieces. Then he found the clean one he had bought for Leslie. 'Write it on this, will you?' He handed her the programme and his pencil and said: 'Good night, good night,' to two more of the cast while he waited. Elizabeth scribbled her address and then, seeing his preoccupied air, wrote something underneath.

Having done that she held out the programme to him, but his attention was fixed furtively upon the door of one of the star dressing-rooms. It was open and a number of people had just come out and were saying good night to Philippa Shelley, who was still in her Japanese costume but had discarded her wig and shaken out her own hair.

'Here you are, Nick,' Elizabeth said.

'Er – thanks,' Talbot answered, taking the programme and stuffing it into his pocket without glancing at it.

'I'd like your help,' Elizabeth said, fingering the pencil and trying to regain his attention. 'Truly. It's not just "one of my tricks".'

Then she saw that the crowd were dispersing, but that Philippa Shelley had seen Nick and instead of going back into her dressing-room was coming towards him. Almost at once Elizabeth jumped at the truth.

'Had I better go?' she asked, under her breath.

'No, of course not,' Nick said.

'Oh, Nick,' said Philippa pleasantly, smiling at him as she came up, 'I think we shall need an extra taxi for the flowers. I was wondering if they'd keep better here till morning. . . . Er . . .' She glanced at Elizabeth.

Nick said: 'This is an old friend of mine, Philippa. We met quite by accident. May I introduce you to my wife, Elizabeth.' He glanced suddenly from one to the other. 'Or have you already met?'

He thought he had caught a glance of recognition pass between them, but in fact it was recognition of another kind, recognition of an implacable understanding instantly formed.

'No, we haven't met,' Philippa said, her eyes a shade cooler. 'How d'you do, Miss – er—'

'Rusman, Elizabeth Rusman. How d'you do, Miss Shelley. I'd no idea you were Nicky's wife. . . . I thought you sang beautifully tonight.'

'Thank you. You're very kind. You were – in the orchestra?'

'I'm afraid as a deputy only. Yes, I knew Nicky well a few years ago. It doesn't seem as long as that, does it?' She appealed to him.

'It seems a long time to me,' he said.

Elizabeth laughed. 'That's very nice of you, Nick.'

Deliberately or accidentally she had turned his words round to mean the opposite.

'The war has upset so many things,' she went on slyly. 'Almost everyone's plans went awry. I know mine did. You're very lucky, Miss Shelley.'

'Thank you,' said Philippa, not showing any special gratification.

'Have you been married long?' Elizabeth asked.

Nick said: 'Yes. Quite a good while.'

Philippa had glanced at her husband. 'D'you mind if I drag Nick away?' she said to the other girl. 'I expect you're tired as well. We've had a frightful day.'

'Of course. I quite understand. I was just going.' Elizabeth glanced swiftly at Nick, who had assumed a poker face. 'Good night, Nicky. See you again, I hope? . . . Good night, Miss Shelley.'

She picked up her violin case and moved off with a quick, easy step – a provocative step, Philippa thought – towards the stage door.

Chapter Four

HE WAITED FOR her while she changed, and then they left by taxi for their flat. She made no reference to Elizabeth, and they chatted amiably enough, though not without some restraint on his side. He was irritated by the exceptional bad luck of Elizabeth's sudden appearance, he was annoyed by her sidelong glances and innuendoes, as if what had happened had been last week and not five years ago. Philippa would expect some explanation; so would anyone; but for the life of him he could not begin it. He wanted to make her an apology without seeming to apologize; and he didn't know how to.

There was the pleasant surprise for her of his telephone call; but here again he was tongue-tied. It seemed that he could not tell her this without falling under a suspicion of trying to divert and placate her.

Altogether it was a most peculiar position, for, normally highly strung and full of nervous energy as she was, it was she who was inclined to be edgy after a concert.

For a few moments they were held up in a traffic block, and at that point she suddenly mentioned what he had avoided. It was not, however, in jealousy but in good-tempered mockery that the first question came.

'She's rather pretty, isn't she – Nicky?'

Philippa had never called him Nicky before in her life. 'Who?' he said obstinately.

'Elizabeth.'

'Oh, yes. In a way.'

'Is she one of your old flames?'

Nick felt anger rising in him, fought it, and lost. But

his voice was still quiet when he said: 'As a matter of fact, yes.'

The taxi started with a jerk, and Philippa looked in surprise at her husband's profile temporarily lighted by a passing car. It was not like him to be on his dignity.

'Are we likely to find many of them scattered about London?'

'What makes you imagine that we shall?'

'Well, we've only been in England three weeks.'

Nick said: 'I've not seen or heard of her for five or six years. I'd almost forgotten her.'

It was Philippa's turn, a little offended by his lack of humour, to struggle with the next words on her tongue. But they came out.

'Was that why you were taking her address?'

'Look,' said Nick. 'She came on me quite suddenly. I never *dreamt* of seeing her. I'd no idea she was even in London. What would you want me to do, sock her on the jaw?'

'Oh, no,' said Philippa, really offended now. 'I'm sure you did *quite* the right thing.'

Talbot blew out a deep breath. 'Good Lord, can't you see, I was taking her address simply because she insisted on giving it to me. There was nothing else I could do. I'd no idea you had such a jealous nature.'

'I'd no idea you had such a past.'

He stared out at the traffic. 'When I met you I was twenty-nine. I never told you I was a plaster saint. I never deceived you in the least. You married me with your eyes open.'

'Perhaps it will be as well if I keep them open.'

'Just as you please. You'll imagine more than you'll see.'

They reached their flat and went up to it in silence. There, over the cold supper left for them by Mrs Saunders, Nick took a grip on his own ill humour. It was so childish, so trivial this bickering, and so indefensible on both sides to let it stain the triumph of the evening. Years hence they would remember the ovation of her first appearance at Covent Garden and they would laugh together over the lovers' tiff that Elizabeth Rusman had caused. But it was up to *him, now* at this moment, to make it a laughing matter which shouldn't spoil anything more.

'Well,' he said, feeling somehow that he couldn't get away from a vague pomposity. 'I won't pretend I'm not glad the ordeal's over. All along I was sure, certain; but one couldn't forget the outside chance.'

'Yes,' she said flatly, and went out to fetch the flask of coffee from the kitchen. He was left with his thoughts.

'Would you rather have gone out with the others to celebrate?' he asked when she came back. 'I did suggest it, you know. . . .'

'No,' she replied. 'I see too much of them as it is – especially Vareni.'

'Angelina has a lovely mezzo voice. She's the best talent in the whole company after you. Your duet was the peak of the second act.'

She nodded. 'I know.'

'Not,' he added, 'that I had any doubts after about the first three minutes of the first act. And I don't think you doubted, did you? I never caught a tremor.'

'Well, of course, my voice doesn't give way at the *first* signs of nervousness.'

He looked at her and then began to sip his coffee.

She added: 'I thought perhaps you'd decided I was no good when you walked out in the middle of the first act.

Or was it because you'd caught sight of Elizabeth Rusman in the orchestra?'

He put down his coffee and got up.

'You are a silly little cat,' he said, and went into the bedroom.

They had never quarrelled like this before. It was nothing, a storm in a teacup, a harmless bickering; and yet it was in danger of becoming everything.

His management of her affairs had become, almost unsought, his chief preoccupation since his demobilization. For him it was an entirely new form of livelihood, but he was convinced that he must continue in it if she was to reach the very top of her profession.

In a sense, in his kindly perception of her finely strung nerves, he had spoiled her, loving her so well and handsomely bending his will to hers, conscious underneath of his own influence, but using it with delicacy and tact. He had met this young singer and fallen deeply in love with her – feeling for her something he had never remotely felt for anyone before – and it was his pleasure and his wish to share in her triumphs, to share her with an acclaiming public and to protect her from such trials and misfortunes as her profession might bring.

But this evening he was out of step. Elizabeth's reappearance had left him irritable and humourless and defensive. He knew that with Elizabeth engaged for at least a week there would be other confoundedly awkward meetings. He would have liked to talk it all over calmly and pleasantly with Philippa, feeling that Philippa was on his side, not ranged against him. He could *not* be kind and tolerant and apologetic.

She came into the bedroom, changed into a scarlet tailored house coat and sat at the dressing-table putting cream on her face. He lay on one of the beds smoking and pretending to read.

There was silence for some time until two fire engines went past, when Philippa, who had been staring at the elephant he'd bought her, said on a more palliative note, oh, she was tired, and what a noisy flat this was, there would be traffic rumbling outside again by seven. Nick, knowing the endless pains Joan had been at to get them the flat on a short lease, pointed out that there was still a housing shortage. He did not point it out angrily or tartly, but he pointed it out.

Philippa splashed a little skin lotion in each palm.

'You seem very much out of sorts tonight, Nick.'

'On the contrary. I've never felt better in my life.'

'Perhaps,' she said, 'you don't like me to surprise you making an appointment with one of your earlier lady friends. I'm sorry, but you should choose somewhere less public than just outside my dressing-room door with all my friends looking on.'

'I'll remember next time,' he told her.

There was silence while Philippa watched him through the glass, her lovely hazel eyes a little perplexed and troubled. But he made no move of reconciliation and, moth to flame, she could not leave it alone.

'Have you known her long?' she asked.

'Who, Elizabeth? No. I told you, I haven't seen her for five years.'

'Did you know her long before that?'

'About three months.'

'Only three months?'

'Anything strange in that?'

'No,' she said, 'except that it seems a short time for working up to a violent love affair.'

'Does it?' He sat up and walked slowly across to the

bathroom. 'No, I don't think so,' he added judiciously as he went out.

She heard the water running. Presently he came back wiping his hands on a towel.

'I've been wondering,' Philippa said.

'What now?'

'Are you any good at mathematics?'

He stared angrily at her. 'Why?'

She said: 'I've been working it out. If we meet one of your discarded mistresses every three weeks of our stay in England, it'll work out at nearly twenty a year.'

'Well, my God!' he exploded. 'This conversation – makes – me – sick!'

He rolled the towel into a ball and flung it at her.

A corner of the towel flicked her face, but the body of it hit the bottle of lotion, which fell over on the dressing-table before her and the contents flooded into her lap.

She stood up, stared at him with angry tears welling into her eyes. Then she snatched up the empty bottle of lotion and threw it at him. It burst like a bomb against the wall beside his head and cascaded him with broken glass.

He stared at her, a startled expression in his eyes, a thin line on his temple slowly turning red and becoming blood.

She was the first to move then, starting forward, her anger quite gone.

'*Nick!* I . . .'

But an anger, rare in him and the more dangerous, had already followed his surprise. He turned his back on her and took a handkerchief from his pocket to dab at his head.

She said breathlessly: 'Nick, I'm so very sorry. Listen, I didn't *mean* it to hit you. You know that.'

Without a word he walked past her into the bathroom. He turned on the tap and damped his handkerchief.

She had followed him. 'Let me look, Nick, please. Is it a deep cut? I'm terribly sorry. Perhaps I could . . .'

'Will you kindly leave me alone,' he said. He had not begun to undress, and he pushed past her, went back into the bedroom to get two clean handkerchiefs and then went through to the living-room and took down his coat and hat.

She stood in the door of the bedroom. 'Darling, do be sensible and let me see. Nick, *please*. You know I never *meant* to hit you. Where are you *going*?'

If he had looked at her then, with her expression so concerned and entreating, he might have stayed and all would have been different. But instead he opened the outer door of the flat and her last appealing 'Nick!' was half inaudible in the banging of the door as he left.

Chapter Five

ELIZABETH RUSMAN did not go straight home, but had
a bite of supper at one of the little cafés in Soho. There
would be nothing to eat when she got home and, besides,
tonight she was excited. First there had been the luck of
her job with the opera, thanks to Mr Till who had be-
friended her; four years out of the professional world and
then a tip-top offer within a month of trying to get back
into it; thank God for influenza. Then there was Nick.
She'd been down on her luck and down in the mouth,
never more so; she'd sat in her miserable bed-sitting-
room and thought what a mess she'd made of her life:
taken all the bad chances and missed all the good. Thirty-
one next month and heartily sick of herself and everyone
else; figure broadening a bit, skin not quite so fine as a
few years ago; she was that sort, fond of the wrong foods.
On her own again and sick of it after only a month.
Sometimes she'd looked at the smutty gas-ring in the fireplace and thought extravagant thoughts about turning it
on and shutting the windows. That would be one way.
But she knew really she'd never have the guts for that. Besides, nobody would be sorry. Nobody would lose a
night's sleep. Nobody would suffer. And she meant somebody to suffer.

Well, her luck had changed today. She was on the up-
grade again. It was so nice to feel that one could be quite
independent in this way whatever the outcome of other
things. And Nick. And Nick. He was most important of
all. She was alive and tingling to her finger-tips after meeting him. And she would see him again. However much he

might try to avoid her, she would be bound to see him again. And after a while perhaps he would no longer try to avoid her. She shut her eyes to the bitter thought that he was married. It had to be ignored. When you got in a mess it was really only a question of keeping going, pegging away, stonewalling until something turned up. Now something had turned up.

She paid for her meal and left the café, and the man with the dark trilby hat watched her go from across the street. She walked home, not begrudging a taxi if she had felt like it, but content with her spreading thoughts.

Loften Street is a long shabby brick cleft in the strata of western London. Featureless except for a few eating houses – '*Pop's Parlour; Steak and Chips 11d.*' – a draper's shop, and two public houses from which now and again shouting women are escorted by patient policemen, it stretches its mean length from one of London's busiest thoroughfares at its east end to a neighbourhood of expensive residential flats at the other. Dry and drab as a bone to the casual eye, there is enough of the rich marrow of human experience behind its shabby curtains to occupy an English Zola for the length of his natural life.

No. 46 is nearer the west end and nearly opposite the smaller of the two public houses. The rain had turned to a fine grey mist as Elizabeth went in, glancing a moment half-defensively towards the sub-basement sitting-room where Mr and Mrs Grieve were usually on watch. There was a light and the door was half open, but nobody was to be seen. She hastened up the first flight of stairs, for if Mike Grieve was there alone he might come out and begin one of his leering conversations.

The 15-watt bulb on the landing was still burning – a sure sign that Mrs Grieve was out – and the sour smell of

34

cooked greens followed her up to the second flight and into her room.

From the first day she had hated it, everything about it: the mirror on the mantelshelf, cracked across the corner, ornate with faded gilt; the big iron bedstead with the ends like prison bars; the dirty lace curtains falling from window-top to floor; the imitation Japanese bric-à-brac; the carpet with the hole where one caught one's foot; the view through the window to a warehouse with wooden platforms for lowering goods into drays in the alley below.

But tonight all this did not seem to matter so much. She would soon be out of here. She pushed the door to behind her with her foot and pulled off her coat and hat, fluffed out her long dark hair, and sat on the bed. There was no sound from above and she remembered that the Allisottis were away for the week visiting an aunt, so she might expect an undisturbed night. And she needed it. All this day had been tiring. She lay back and closed her eyes.

She opened them at the sound of a knock.

'Come in,' she said, forgetting Mike Grieve.

A man came in.

She sat up. Her eyes changed their expression, drowsiness fled before surprise. Startled, wary, suddenly hostile, she slipped off the bed and stood up.

'What do you want?' she demanded.

The swing door of the public house opposite opened suddenly to emit a gust of laughter and Mike Grieve.

He staggered a little as he came out, not because he was drunk – he couldn't afford that at present – but because four of his friends had given him a hearty shove as he reached the door to make sure that he went home in style. The force of his going had made him spill some of the froth out of the quart jug he was carrying, and as he walked towards his own door he changed hands to lick the beer off his fingers.

Ma Grieve had gone to see her mother, but would be back about eleven, and it would be more than his life was worth to be found in the White Horse while the lodgings were unattended. It might be Buckingham Palace and the Crown Jewels the way she watched over it, afraid of someone pinching off without paying the rent, Mr Allisotti always said, when Ma wasn't around.

Mike reached the door safely and was about to turn down into their own room when he saw someone coming down the ill-lit stairs. He drew aside to let the man pass. He was a stranger and wore a mackintosh and a dark trilby hat. He had a handkerchief held to his face and kept his head well down.

'Good night, guv'nor,' said Mike, feeling friendly.

'Night,' the stranger said, passing Mike on the handkerchief side.

' 'Urt yer 'ead?' Mike asked solicitously, but he had no reply. The stranger passed on and went out into the street. There the damp mist swallowed him.

Grieve grunted and went down into the sitting-room. He had forgotten to switch off the electric, but he had only meant to slip out for a minute, not stay half an hour. Good job Ma hadn't come home early.

He picked up the paper and began to read the racing form, his feet on the table, his left hand stretching out now and then for the mug of beer. When he finished a draught his bottom lip came out and sucked the beads of dampness off his drooping moustache.

But after a moment or two he put down the paper and stared at the photograph of himself as a virile young man on the opposite wall. The Allisottis were away this week

36

and the second floor front hadn't been let since Old Man
Thomas walked out. Third floor back, Hartley, was on
night shift. That left only Miss Rusman. What was she
doing having gentlemen friends at near on midnight?

Well, it was hardly his business. Mike was all for toler-
ance. He'd tell Ma, who wasn't, and let her worry. He
picked up the paper again but did not read it. It was
hardly his business, but the Rusman girl, sawing away at
her violin, with her stuck-up airs and her sulky mouth as
if ordinary folk wasn't good enough for her. . . . The way
she'd acted to him. 'I'm not interested in what you think
or feel, Mr Grieve. Kindly get out of this bedroom or I'll
call the police.' And she *had* called young Hartley, who
happened to be passing. Flag-flying, haughty little so-and-
so. And now it seemed that after all she was no better than
a high-class what's it. Men coming out of her room late at
night. He'd a mind to go up and see what it was all about.

Perhaps tonight she wouldn't look on things in quite
the same way. Anyway, she'd better not come the high
and mighty now. He stared at his own photo again. A
pity Ma would be back any minute. But he'd a fair excuse
for going upstairs. Ma wouldn't have any funny business
going on in her house. He knew that well enough, for she
was always saying so.

He'd go and have a little talk with Miss Rusman.

He drained his beer and sucked the ends of his moustache and got up. Outside, the clock of St Andrew's
Church by the market was just striking eleven.

As he reached the first landing he was about to switch
out the light but thought he would leave it till he came
down, otherwise he might catch his head on the bracket.
He'd done it before. He wondered if the stranger had
banged his head there.

He puffed up to the second landing, looking out for the

creaking boards, and approached the door of the second floor back. No sound. Maybe she was in bed. That seemed very likely. But not asleep. He raised his hand to knock.

His nostrils twitched. Funny smell. She must be cooking something on the gas-ring and it had boiled over. Or . . .

He knocked. No reply.

He switched on the other light on the landing and saw smoke curling unpretentiously round the bottom of the door.

He turned the handle sharply and found the door was not locked. A cloud of smoke came out and made him choke. Then he went in.

The bed was on fire.

Something dark was lying on the bed.

He lost his head and ran back upon the landing, calling, 'Help! Help!' down the stairs.

But it was no good shouting when he was alone in the house – except for whatever lay in that room. The bed was on fire, the window curtains smoking: those curtains Ma was so proud of.

He began to swear and cry out, waving his hands as if there was someone to see, while in there he knew the flames were crackling at him – leaping and vanishing in smoke, and licking and leaping again.

Then his wits returned and he swung round and plunged back clumsily into the blazing room.

Nick Talbot had been walking for hours – or so it seemed. The mist was a bit thicker and he had lost his bearings. The cut on his forehead had dried for a while, but now it had broken out afresh. He had thought several times of going home, but each time his feelings had stopped him. Now, when he would gladly have gone home and put an end to the quarrel, he could not find his way. He had wandered into a poor district and as usual when one was wanted there was not a sign of a taxi.

Under the white vapour of a street light he stared at the handkerchief with which he had been dabbing his forehead and saw fresh blood on it.

A few yards back he had passed a small chemist's shop with a lighted sign on the door. He turned back and went in.

The shop bell clanged, and after a moment a thin, spectacled, furtive man stood up behind the counter dusting cigarette ash off his sleeves.

'Yes?' he said in an uncharitable voice.

'I want you to look at my forehead. I've had a slight accident.'

The chemist came round on creaking shoes.

'Hm. Bend down. Under the light, will you?'

He examined the cut, sniffing for the smell of whisky on his customer's breath.

'I can't do anything to *that*. Did you fall?'

'Er – yes. This mist, you know.'

The man smiled humourlessly.

'Well, it's more than I can manage. You'll need a stitch or two.'

Nick shifted. 'Can't you make it stop bleeding?'

'Sorry, no. I wouldn't touch it. You'd be left with a nasty scar. It's not in my line. The Fitzroy Street Hospital is just around the corner. There's always a night staff there.'

'Which way do I go?'

'First on the left, and first on the left again. Two minutes' walk, that's all.'

'Thank you,' Talbot said, picking up his hat.

39

The fire had been out twenty minutes, but there was still a thin ceiling of smoke in the room. The acrid smell of burnt blankets and leather was not quite strong enough to drown a more unpleasant smell. Everything was disordered, ornaments lay in the fireplace, chairs were overturned. There were people about the room, Mike Grieve sitting in a corner telling it all a third time to a sergeant of police with a bad cold, another policeman by the half-open door. Something still lay on the bed covered by a half-burnt sheet.

Through the door came the voice of Ma Grieve on a monotonous note of complaint.

'Always when I go out. Why wasn't I 'ere? Why wasn't I 'ere? If you leave '*im* in charge, well, you can always depend on it . . . Always somefing. Only last week Mr Allisotti overflowed the bath . . .'

A second constable came into the room, a little short of breath with the stairs.

'Inspector Archer's here, Sergeant. And the Divisional Surgeon. They've made quick time.'

'Good,' said the sergeant, pushing back his big hat, and blew his nose.

Footsteps sounded, and Inspector Archer came in with Dr Frederick at his heels. Archer was a big tidy man going grey; he looked like a respectable merchant with a wife and five children in Hammersmith. He had deep-set eyes and rather small soft hands with the nails cut close.

The sergeant got up, putting away his handkerchief. ''Morning, sir. 'Morning. We've been careful to touch nothing. Beyond, that is, what we were forced to handle making sure the fire was out. And the corpse . . .'

'All through the blitz,' came Mrs Grieve's voice. 'Not a window broke. Only one perishin' fire-bomb on the roof. An' now this. It makes you curdle. . . .'

Archer said: 'Who's this man?'

'The landlord. He says he was out at the time.'

' 'Course I was out,' Grieve said sulkily. 'There's twenty people at the White Horse can prove it.'

'Get the stairs cleared, will you,' said Archer. 'People back in their own rooms and onlookers out of the house.'

They moved over to the bed. Delicately, with finger and thumb, Archer pulled back a corner of the sheet. He pursed his lips a little with a moue of distaste. Dr Frederick pulled the sheet right back. They bent to examine the body.

There was silence for a time.

Then Grieve shifted in his seat and said: 'He'd mebbe be about six foot, this man. " 'Night," I says to him, me being civil. " 'Night," he says. That's all. Then out he goes with his 'and to his 'ead.'

Archer turned from the body and glanced at Grieve with narrowed assessing eyes. He seemed to take the speaker in from head to foot.

'What's this about a man?'

The sergeant told him.

Archer continued to stare at Grieve. 'What's wrong with your hands?'

'Scorched 'em putting out the fire. So has my missus. She came in just as I was putting of it out.'

'Did she see this man?'

'Lord, no. He was gone afore ever I come up the stairs.'

'Would you recognize him again?'

'Mebbe. I didn't see 'is face all that plain: but mebbe I'd reckernize him if I was to see 'im close.'

The inspector took a deep thoughtful breath and allowed it slowly to escape as his glance came back to the notes the sergeant had offered him. Then he turned to the doctor, who had straightened up.

'Well, Frederick?'

'She's been dead about half an hour,' Frederick said in a low voice. 'I think she's been strangled.'

Archer's eyes wandered round the room. 'Looks as if there was a bit of a struggle, eh?'

'Lucky the fire was put out. In another ten minutes it would have destroyed everything.'

Archer's eyes rested again on Grieve, then passed on. 'Badly burned, isn't she?'

'Features and hair, yes. She might be difficult to identify.'

'Fortunately that will only be a formality. Hm, Mr Grieve, how long has this Miss Rusman been with you?'

'Three weeks last Friday. That's all. Never seen her afore then. Never seen her. Don't know where she comes from nor nothing.'

'Is there a telephone near here?'

'Next door, sir,' said one of the constables. 'That's where I telephoned from.'

'Well, take this description, have it circulated, see. Get it round as soon as possible to all hospitals, etc. There's just a chance it might help. . . . It's a long chance, but still . . .'

'Yes, sir.' The constable went out. Archer plucked at his lip.

'Where's her case?' he said. 'Her belongings and things.'

'Most of them have been burnt,' the sergeant said, pointing to a mass of ashes and charred material behind the bed.

'Wonder if they went by accident or design. Sergeant, you'd better get this man out of here.'

'There's this,' said Dr Frederick. 'It was round her neck. It looks as if it might open.'

Archer stared at the little gold heart-shaped locket. He tried to get his broad thumbnail into a possible nick. Then he saw a press-catch as small as a pin-head and squeezed it. The locket swung open on hinges.

Inside was a small photograph of the head and shoulders of a man. It was not very clear, but quite clear enough to be circulated and to be recognizable if by any chance the police should catch up with him.

He had found the 'night staff', and the worst was over. At least the two stitches were in, and this harsh stinging would stop in time.

An elderly porter with a stiff leg had let him in, grudgingly, through a very-slow-widening crack in the door, and then had led him in a cloud of strong tobacco smoke up a long stone passage and into a room where they had found a young nurse and a younger doctor just finishing a meal of scrambled eggs and coffee. The doctor, called Harris, and the nurse, called Green, had quickly put on a professional manner, through which their youth and inexperience continued to stick out like bones through an ill-fitting coat.

While the business was in process he had refrained, in the interests of his own peace of mind, from asking too many questions – it was better not to know than to know what he wryly suspected – but at this stage he said:

'Done this job before?'

'What?' said the doctor, looking up quickly. 'What d'you mean?'

'This your first accident casualty?'

'Good Lord, no. What makes you think that?'

Nick said: 'You're very young. I thought you couldn't have been at the job long.'

'Over six weeks now.'

Nick winced slightly. 'Think you've made a nice neat darn of it?'

'Lovely,' said Dr Harris, and glanced idly at the nurse as she left the room. 'Couldn't have done it better if I'd got my fellowship. As pretty a job as I ever saw. There was no glass in the wound, by the way. Did you say it was a car accident?'

Talbot had mumbled the first excuse that had come into his head.

'Taxi skidded into a lamp standard,' he said discouragingly.

But the young doctor was not curious. 'Lucky you didn't overturn. I was in a little M.G. sports once on the Brighton road. We were taking a corner at about sixty-eight when a tyre burst. Lucky for us—'

Nurse Green had come back. 'You're wanted on the phone.'

'Who, me?' said the doctor. 'Who wants me?'

'They didn't say.'

'Lucky for us there were no cars ahead,' said Harris, retreating towards the door. 'We skidded twice round without taking a wheel off the road, went through a gate and ran into a cow. It stopped us dead. A good piece of driving, you know.'

'What happened to the cow?' asked Nick.

'Oh, the farmer was insured,' said the young man as he disappeared.

Nick was left to think about Philippa for a few moments. Fitzroy Street was not really so far from the flat and he could be home in under ten minutes. Put an end to this silly squabble once and for all. . . .

'Can I pay for this job?' he said to the nurse, who was tidying up on the table.

'No, thanks, it's on the house.' She smiled. 'But there's a box for the Waifs and Strays at the door as you go out – that's if you feel inclined.'

Talbot smiled back at her. 'Right. Thank you.'

Harris came back. He came slowly in, shutting the door after him, and slowly across in the direction of Nick.

'Anything important?' asked the nurse.

'Um? Oh . . . er – no. No, nothing much.' The young man looked absent-minded. In a queer voice he said to Talbot: 'Let's see; where was I?'

'You'd just killed a cow,' Nick said.

'Yes. . . . Ha, ha! Yes, I had, hadn't I? Well, I tell you we were – er – lucky, don't you think, to get off without even – er – a cut finger. Luckier than you, and I expect – er – our crash was much more of a crash than yours.' He gazed hopefully at Nurse Green, who gazed back at him.

There was a moment's unproductive silence.

'Yes, we were certainly lucky,' said Harris, clinching the matter.

'Suppose you finish this bandage,' Nick reminded him gently.

'Yes. Oh, yes.' The young surgeon moved over to him and seemed somehow more confident now that he had his fingers on his patient's head. 'Let me see. Better put on a bit more to keep it quite dry. Pass me the bandage, nurse.'

'Don't you think—'

But he interrupted her. 'Pass me the bandage, please.'

Patiently, and with no more said, Nick accepted another wrapping.

But if Dr Harris had seemed faintly uncertain before, now his fingers were really clumsy and unprofessional. First he got the bandage on and then apparently did not like the look of it, for he unwound it again and began afresh. Even this did not satisfy him, and presently Talbot began to stir under his treatment. What did it matter whether the thing was just so? Philippa herself would make a better job of it when he got home: she had done lots of such work in the camp where she had been interned so long.

'Don't forget I want to get my hat on,' he said, rising at last. 'Thank you very much for all your help.' He glanced at Nurse Green's flushed face. 'What's the matter?'

'Nothing,' she said. 'Nothing at all.'

'Best thing we can do,' Harris said, 'is to telephone for a taxi for you. Then you can be driven straight home.'

Nick felt his bandages. It seemed a good job after all. 'Thanks, I'll walk. The rain has stopped.'

'Oh, you shouldn't do that. Worst thing possible after shock.'

'I'll risk it.'

He was moving towards the door when the doctor said:

'Just a moment. There's a frayed end to the bandage. I'll cut it off.'

Impatiently Nick suffered this last attention; and while it was being done there was the sound of a car drawing up outside. Because they were so close together he caught a curious effect of the doctor's breathing, as if breath which had been held was being slowly let out.

'Another casualty?' Nick asked, gingerly trying on his hat.

The question was met with a cautious smile. 'Perhaps it's going to be a busy night.'

Nick said: 'Well, I'll make way for the next case. Thanks a lot for your help.'

He went to the door and turned into the long stone passage. As he did so the door opened at the other end and the porter came limping along in company with two other men. One was a uniformed policeman.

They met half-way down and seemed to fill the passage.

'Good evening,' said one man, looking beyond Nick, 'Are you Dr Harris?'

Nick half turned and saw that the young surgeon had followed him.

'Yes,' said Harris. 'Yes. I . . . you telephoned and I thought . . .'

'Very good of you. Thanks. Pardon me a moment, sir.'

Nick, thinking this none of his business, had moved to go past, but somehow the policeman got in his way.

'Yes?' said Nick impatiently.

'Could I trouble you a moment?' said the other man. He was polite, even casual in his manner, but underlying it was a hint of authority. Inspector Archer was glad he had decided to come on this mission, which might so easily have proved a wild-goose chase. He was certain it was not that now, for he had recognized this tall man as the man whose photograph he had just found in the murdered woman's locket.

Philippa had slept very little during the night. She had waited up until two, hoping every minute that Nick would come back. Once she thought she heard his footsteps on the landing and had gone to the door and peered down the empty stairs.

Very early on in the night she had realized that if there is to be a true honest unreserved making up of a quarrel, the only way is to forget what possible offence the other person has given you and think only how bad you've been yourself. That was not hard. Last night there had grown up inside her a devil of contrariness. Joyous at her own success, entirely in love with her husband, she had let these ugly growths run the evening into ruin. Nerves didn't quite explain it. Pride didn't explain it. Elizabeth Rusman didn't quite explain it. It was a paradox of life, she told herself, because these ill things had grown out of her *happiness*. She would not have been so over-strung with a more moderate success, she would not have been nearly so bitter towards Nick if she had not loved him so much.

But she was clear-sighted enough to see how hard it might be to put things right. Into the pillow or outward to the empty air she could say she was sorry with all frankness and abandon. Facing him would be more difficult. The perversities would still put obstacles in her way, make her tongue hesitate, qualify the sincerity of her apology. No doubt they'd tempt some remark to his lips to try to turn all her good intentions to waste.

Well, she would see. It was a matter of pride now, pride in herself. Absolute apology there should be, and nothing should stop her.

Before lying down she had been specially careful to tidy up all signs of the quarrel; it seemed important to her. She had washed out her own things which were stained by the lotion – luckily her expensive house coat had escaped – she had brushed up the broken glass and carried it downstairs to the central heating stove which served all the flats. It all gave her something to do, to occupy her hands if not her mind.

But he did not come. She had not imagined he would stay out the whole night like this. Perhaps he had gone to his sister's. But no, he'd never do that. It had been a principle of theirs from the start. If they ever quarrelled it was a private thing between themselves, kept to themselves. He would never tell any third person. Then where was he? At some hotel? How bad had the injury been? Glass could cut deep. He couldn't surely have fainted somewhere and have lain there unseen . . .? Or been taken to a hospital? They would have let her know. Perhaps he had told them not to. He had papers on him.

By six sleep was hopeless and she got up and went into the kitchen to brew some tea. She was glad she was not singing tonight. She would have a chance of relaxing before Wednesday. The triumph of last night seemed a mockery. She didn't seem to care what the papers said. . . . If . . .

There was a knock on the outer door.

Startled, she hurried through the living-room, wondering what she would find. Nick had a key. But he might have lost it. Or there might be . . .

Two strangers were standing there. One, a heavy man in a neat dark suit, was newly shaven and looked tired; the other was taller and younger with a sort of facile eagerness in his glance.

She stepped back.

'Mrs Nicolas Talbot?'

'Yes.'

'I beg your pardon for disturbing you at this hour. I'm Divisional Inspector Archer of the Metropolitan Police.'

The floor seemed suddenly nearer to Philippa, and she took a firmer grip of the door. They did not seem to have noticed her movement.

'Come in,' she said.

As they went past her she found she could not wait. She said to the older man:

'What is it? Nick – has anything happened to my husband?'

'No, no,' said Archer conventionally. 'Nothing at all, Mrs Talbot. We're just making a few inquiries and thought you could help us.'

She watched them stand in the middle of the room,

49

waiting, tall and unconformable, for her to sit down. She found the edge of a chair, trying instinctively to hide her nightdress.

Archer cleared his throat.

'Do you know a Miss Elizabeth Rusman, Mrs Talbot?'

She stared back at him in astonishment.

'I met her for the first time last night. Why?'

'Well, she's dead,' said Archer, watching her, while the thin sharp man licked the end of his thin sharp pencil.

Philippa said: 'But only last night . . .' Her mind jumped on to a suicide. 'Was Nick . . . ? Does Nick know about this?'

'You think it likely that he should?'

'Only if you've told him.'

Archer's deep-looking eyes had been taking stock of her, of her tall, slender, resilient figure, of her young fair beauty, with all its pride and grace and high-strung excellence. But this morning they meant no more to him than any other fact to be docketed in his tidy mind. The physical appeal of this young woman was, or might become, a numeral, a letter, a symbol in the formula which would one day spell out the solution of Elizabeth Rusman's murder.

'If it's not a rude question, Mrs Talbot, how long have you been married?'

'Twelve months.'

'Have you been in England much of that time?'

'No, we arrived only three weeks ago.'

Archer smiled suddenly, turning it on with the facial muscles to be reassuring. 'I know you'll forgive me if these questions seem impertinent. As a police officer, you know, one gets so used . . .' He turned off the smile. 'Are you happy in your married life?'

Philippa made a little moue of embarrassment. 'Well, I
. . . of course. Completely. Very happy indeed.'

'Did you quarrel with your husband last night?'

There was a fractional hesitation while her mind weighed
up the question. What *did* they want?

'No,' she said, old instinct carrying the day. 'Why do
you ask?'

The inspector's eyes moved round the room.

'You're a singer, aren't you, Mrs Talbot? Opera, I believe? What time did you get home last night? Can you
remember?'

'A little before ten, I think.'

'Did your husband come home with you?'

She got to her feet. 'What's the matter? Tell me what's
the matter!'

'I don't want you to be alarmed,' Archer said. 'But we
think Elizabeth Rusman was murdered. Certain facts link
your husband with the matter and we think he may be
able to help us. He's been detained at Bow Street for
questioning.'

Chapter Six

MR FROBISHER carefully looked at his clerk.

'Mrs Talbot? Do I know her? Was she the lady waiting when I came in? Ask Mr Forbes if he'll see Mr Smith when he comes.'

Philippa was shown in.

'Why, Miss Shelley,' said Mr Frobisher, rising. 'I didn't recognize you. Of course, it must be six years. You're Mrs Talbot now?'

Philippa shook hands with him. 'I came to you, Mr Frobisher; I happened to remember your address and you were the only solicitor I knew. You see, I thought I'd prefer to talk this over with someone.'

'Do sit down. Some trouble? Don't hurry yourself. Have you been married long?'

It took some minutes for Philippa to tell Mr Frobisher all he wanted to know about her career; he had known her as a girl of eighteen struggling to make enough money to pay for music lessons abroad. Urgency prompted her to cut him short and to tell him of last night, of Nick's meeting with Elizabeth Rusman. Shame made her try to minimize the quarrel, to make it seem half horse-play; her face flushed up as she spoke of throwing the bottle of lotion, of Nick's walking out, of the visit from the police this morning.

'They seem to imagine Nick may know something about it! The janitor of the lodgings where Elizabeth Rusman was staying described a man he had seen coming out just before she – she was discovered, and they telephoned this description round to hospitals. He'd hurt his face or was holding a handkerchief to it or something. Well, Nick must have gone into a hospital to have his head dressed, and with this description before them they telephoned the police, and the police arrested him just as he was leaving. It's completely fantastic! I – I haven't known what to do for the best. It's seemed like half a day waiting for you to come. . . .'

Mr Frobisher carefully smoothed back his stiff grey hair. His scholarly cautious legal mind went all round the situation, like a cat round a piece of fish, before picking it up.

'I can understand that. Well understand it. Possibly it is just an unfortunate coincidence. The fact of his being in the neighbourhood at the time; the misfortune of his knowing the dead woman. If so, there's no doubt we shall soon be able to straighten it out. Where is your husband?'

'Bow Street.'

'Well, I think we should go there at once. When we get all the facts we shall be in a better position to act.'

Archer looked at Talbot across the table. He gazed at him without animosity but without favour. Not at all the usual type to be brought in here: the trickster, the petty burglar, the drunk, the disorderly, the pickpocket or the pimp. (The small crimes were so much more numerous than the big, and even the big were usually committed by the small man getting above himself.) Educated men there were in here, but usually they were down-at-heel, suavely apologetic, or arrogant, overfed, uneasy, blustering. Public schoolboys were not a type Archer really approved of. Having worked his way up from nothing with laborious, intelligent application, he did not appreciate the man who started half-way up the ladder for other reasons than pure

53

merit. He found himself at a disadvantage with them in his own profession, and although twenty years of varied experience had given him all the confidence he could need in dealing with a lawbreaker of any class, he was conscious deep down inside him that he was ever so slightly at a disadvantage with this cool self-contained man who was neither shabby nor suave, nor in any degree apologetic.

For this reason he was conscious of a faint antagonism towards Talbot. And because of this feeling it was necessary that he should treat him with more than ordinary consideration.

'Look, Captain Talbot. This statement you made last night. Here it is; read it over again; I don't wish to take any unfair advantage of you. You'd had a trying evening, to say the least. Now you're rested, no doubt you'd like to add to it, or to amend it.'

'I've no wish to do anything of the sort,' Talbot said, his voice sounding unlike his own in the tiny high room with its cheap magazines and its smell of Jeyes.

'Well, help us to straighten out these contradictory stories then. When you went to the hospital you told them you'd had an accident in a taxi and had been cut by the breaking glass. When we came along you stuck to that story, gave us all sorts of circumstantial details. It was only when we pressed you further that you completely changed your story, said you'd cut your head in a quarrel with your wife. Well, you obviously can't expect us to believe both stories. Which one do you prefer this morning?'

Nick said: 'Are you married yourself, Inspector?'

'Yes.' Archer spoke reluctantly, a little irritated by a question which brought his own personality into it.

'Then surely you must realize the sort of instinct that exists in us all to – to keep our dirty linen for private washing. My wife threw something at me, not really meaning to hit me, but it did. It's only natural I shouldn't want to brag about a thing like that.'

'When we called on your wife this morning she denied ever having had such a quarrel.'

'Well, I'm glad the same instinct was working in her. But when you told her—'

'Nor,' said Archer patiently, 'were there any signs of a quarrel in your flat.'

'What did she say?'

'When we went into further details she then changed her story, supporting your statement and saying that she had cleared everything up. There was no trace of any broken glass and she claimed that during the night she had brushed up this glass and carried it down to the incinerator in the kitchens. There can of course be no proof of this, but naturally every effort will be made to check up on her statement.'

Archer paused and blew out his cheeks.

'And in the meantime?' said Nick.

'In the meantime I'm afraid we shall have to detain you a little longer. Now, you know, we had to go through the formality of examining your pockets when you came here. This programme was among the effects. "A performance of *Madame Butterfly* on Monday the—"'

'Yes. That's mine.'

Archer turned it over. 'On the back we find written "Elizabeth, 46, Loften Street, W.1." Is that your writing?'

Nick shifted on his hard chair. 'No. Miss Rusman wrote that when we happened to meet at the opera last night.'

'I see. And I suppose she wrote the rest, did she?'

The younger man looked up in surprise. 'What do you mean?'

'This.' Archer pointed. ' "Don't fail to come. Alas, the love of women!" '

'Good God.' Talbot frowned. 'Did she put that? I never looked.'

Archer pursed his lips. 'You mean you didn't know it was there?'

Nick was lost for a moment in his own memories. 'Poor little beggar. . . . No, I merely stuffed the programme in my pocket. I didn't know she'd written anything else.'

Archer grunted. He was very tired, and for a moment his mind wandered to his own home in Streatham; a new patch of grass where the vegetables had been, and yesterday morning the first green sprouting.

'Then there are these two letters,' he said, frowning his re-concentration at the deal table. 'Written to the dead woman five years ago and found in the lining of her violin case. Finally, there's this pencil, which you admit to having in your possession as late as yesterday. Yet it was lying on the floor of the room where this young woman was murdered.'

Nick shrugged his shoulders rather hopelessly. 'It's all very unfortunate, I agree. Why she should have kept the letters all this time I can't think. But surely the explanation of the pencil suggests itself? Have you never loaned a pencil for someone to scribble something down and then forgotten to get it back?'

'I'm afraid it's not for us to supply the explanations, Mr Talbot. If that's the truth, then I am just as anxious to establish it as you are. Now I hope you'll not object to taking part in an identity parade? Just nine or ten of you dressed exactly alike in mackintoshes and felt hats.'

'What about this?' Nick fingered the neat bandage on his forehead.'

'Oh, all the others will be bandaged just the same. There'll be nothing to fear on that account.'

The other shrugged again. 'When do we start?'

Archer got up. 'I'll get Sergeant Standish.'

Five minutes later, Nick was standing with nine other strange men, all wearing mackintoshes and all bandaged over the left temple. Yet there was something distinctive about him which seemed to set him apart from the rest. He'd got the stamp of command and the stamp of culture. At a word from the sergeant they all put on dark grey hats and he then went round adjusting them to the same angle. Then they filed out into a big bare room like a polling booth and stood against one wall under the lights.

Three men came in through another door.

There was silence. After a few moments a voice, hoarse with years of beer-drinking, said: 'Can I get a bit nearer, guv'nor?'

One of the men at the other end came half-way down the room, stood there uncertainly, feeling his neck-band, sucking at his moustache.

'Will you all turn round, please,' Archer said.

When they faced the room again the man with the big moustache had come quite close to them and after some moments his eyes fastened on Nick Talbot. Talbot stared back at him bleakly.

'Blimey, I think that's 'im,' Grieve said, pointing. Conviction hardened, hesitation fled. 'Yus, that's 'im. That tall one, guv'nor. That one there. I reckon that's 'im.'

'Are you sure?' Archer was behind him, his tired features tightened up at this moment of decision.

'Yus,' said Grieve. 'That's 'im, I reckon.'

It was all smaller and more shabby than she had expected of the most famous police station in London. The dreary, bare office place with policemen behind the counter; the smell of disinfectant; the little, ragged, dirty man waiting with a smouldering cigarette in his mouth directly under the 'SMOKING PROHIBITED' notice; the noise one's feet made on the tiled floor. It might have been a converted nineteenth-century council school.

As she came in she had seen the bills of the coming night's opera outside the scene of last night's triumph. The two things faced each other in her mind. The patient respectable queue waiting to book seats; the middle-aged tart deliberately getting out of a taxi at the police station and flouncing off down the street under the eyes of the constable at the door. The majesty of success and the majesty of the law.

But last night's was true, worked for through years; this was false, undeserved, would be quickly cast off by common sense. As soon as she saw him she would know it was going to be all right. . . .

As the warder unlocked the door, she tightened her grip on her gloves and wondered what word she should say. But when she went in, and Nick stood up and came towards her, she knew that no word was necessary.

For a few moments they clung to each other, and despite the happiness of the reconciliation she felt at once that this thing was not going to be blown away. She was surprised at the curious strained look in his eyes, the tight little lines about his mouth. She saw the ordeal he had been through, the humiliation and anger and impotence, the first fine threads of fear trying to weave themselves about his mind. He had knocked about the world a good bit, but this was something outside his experience. Like most normal men he had a considerable respect for the law – though he might not betray it to a questioning police officer. He felt this as if he had been brought up on some fake charge for court martial.

'Phil,' he said after a moment.

'Oh, Nick, I . . . It's been like a nightmare. What *is* it all about? Last night—'

'It's just a damned silly mistake,' he said, 'but I don't pretend to be amused.'

'Your head,' she said, glancing up, and the colour coming to her face again.

'Oh, that's all right.' He made a grimace. 'Two stitches at the Fitzroy Street Hospital by a surgeon hardly out of his teens who might have been sewing up his brother's shirt. . . .'

'What happened after you left?'

'I walked and walked, trying to get rid of the spleen that had somehow come between us. For a time the cut stopped bleeding, but then it began again and I went to have it seen to. The surgeon phoned the police, and just as I was leaving this man Archer turned up and began asking questions. It's a complete mystery to me.'

His bitter dejected manner alarmed her.

'Well, it can only be a misunderstanding for a short time. The English police don't make silly mistakes for long. It's unpleasant, but there's no reason to be *really* alarmed.'

'That's what I've been telling myself until a few minutes ago,' he said.

'What d'you mean?'

He shrugged. 'They've had an identity parade. Ten of us up against a wall. Some man from this boarding house where Elizabeth Rusman died thinks he's identified me as a man he saw coming out of her room last night.'

She felt as if something had laid cold fingers on her heart.

'Nick. . . . How could that be. . . ? You didn't go?'

'At that time of night? Of course not. I never wanted to see her again.'

'There must have been someone there like you. A superficial likeness, anyway.'

'You see, it all fits in; the cut forehead and everything.'

'But I can confirm your story of what really happened.'

'Having denied it first, as I did.' Talbot sighed. 'Never in my life, Philippa, have I felt so much like a liar as I did last night when I started telling them the truth about our quarrel. They just stood there with dead-pan faces writing it all down. I believe they'd have respected me more if I'd kept to my accident story.'

'But surely they can't keep you here!' Philippa said. 'What right have they to put you in a cell!'

'It isn't a cell. This is the room where people are detained for questioning. Fortunately I don't get claustrophobia.'

'Won't they release you on bail?'

'Not yet. The thing for us to do now is get a solicitor.' She smiled briefly. 'I'd forgotten. I have one outside.'

He smiled back at her a moment. 'I shall be in good hands with you to look after my interests. Why had this to happen, Philippa? Have you seen your notices? There are two here – they couldn't be better.'

She stared at the paper he was holding out to her. 'After you left last night, Nick, I was so ashamed.'

'Look,' he said. 'You see what Wightman says: 'Continental newcomers, for longer than it is comfortable to remember, have tried to capture our approval with detested tremolos, with taking too short a view of their phrases and with loud and noisy dramatic tantrums which completely ruin their accuracy of pitch. Our joy then last night was the more sincere in finding among this youthful and eager company a soprano who combines round-ness and purity of tone with an overall evenness of scale—'

'I meant to ask you to try to forget what had happened,' she said. 'But it's impossible now, for all this has grown out of it. I must have been mad.'

'We both acted like spoilt children,' he said. 'Which I suppose we are: spoiled by fate. I'm really much the most to blame; I was insufferably irritable and stuffy and pompous. With a dozen words I could have stopped it all.'

'I wasn't really ever seriously jealous of that girl,' she said. 'That's the silly part of it. And I knew very well that you had some good reason for leaving the box which had nothing to do with her.'

'Lou Friedman was on the telephone from New York,' he told her. 'He'd forgotten our operas started so early. He can arrange an American contract for you if this season is a success.'

There was silence for several seconds.

'That makes me feel *very* small,' she said in a low voice.

'Don't you see? And me also. I had only to tell you, to kill the quarrel stone dead.'

'I never gave you a chance.'

He took her face in his hands and kissed her.

'Last night was yesterday, and no good comes of crying over it. It can't be helped. Today we've got to face this boring interlude. Your success is the stable, important thing. This can only put us out for a few days. Somewhere there's another man. They already know he's a bit like me and has a bandaged head. They're bound to trace him pretty quickly. Now let's have this lawyer in and see what he has to suggest.'

As she went to the door she was thinking: a man with an injured head and murder on his conscience will lie low, desperately low, fox in hole, hiding his hurt at any cost, while another man takes the suspicion and the consequences.

Chapter Seven

Two and a half miles away, Mr Sidney Fleming was trying out his handwriting. He sat at a desk in his hotel bedroom – with its well-worn hair-cord carpet, its chromium fittings, its shabbily genteel eiderdown – and the pile of half-burnt cigarettes in the ash-tray and the scattered sheets of notepaper showed the difficulties he had been put to.

Yet to look at him one would have thought him an intelligent and educated man.

'Dear Dr Wishart,' he began laboriously for the seventh time. 'I am writing to tell you . . .'

He was interrupted by a rap on the door and the rattle of a master key in the lock. Quickly he picked up a newspaper and dropped it over the letters. He stood up as a porter came in. The porter blinked uncertainly at his back.

'You've got some luggage, haven't you, sir?'

'You're early,' snapped Fleming. 'I told them eleven-thirty.'

'Oh . . . sorry . . .' The man turned to go out.

'Wait,' said Fleming. 'You can take that. I'll bring the small case. Here.' He handed the man a coin, without properly turning to face him.

'Thank you, sir,' said the porter more affably.

'And get me a taxi at eleven-thirty. I've a train to catch.'

'Yes, sir.' The man went out.

Fool! Why be frightened of three pieces of sticking-plaster? – it isn't even in the papers yet. Why tell the porter needlessly about catching a train? Why be irritable and edgy? Because twelve hours ago exactly you were stopping the flow of blood to her brain and air to her lungs; brown kid gloves on the smooth white throat, which wasn't really smooth at all when you pressed into the bone and the sinew and the veins. How she'd struggled, the bitch; he'd known of course she was strong. He'd never have had the anger to kill her if she'd kept quiet; it would have fizzled out like a damp squib in spite of all she'd said and meant to do; his anger was like that, peaks and valleys; but she'd fought and kicked and tried to scream; he was bruised and blue and had been sick a couple of streets away.

He turned back to the table, fingering his head.

Another letter. 'Dear Mrs MacArdle,' he began this time; and went right through to the end. It was better; yes, it would do, would have to. His watch – it was eleven-fifteen; sweat broke on his face; a quarter of an hour and the hardest yet to write.

Desperation gave him courage and he finished the second with a few minutes to spare. He addressed, stamped and sealed both, stuffed the wasted pieces of notepaper into his case and looked around. He picked up the ash-tray and emptied half the ends out of the window on to the lead roof beneath. He looked round again. No blood on the pillow. He'd had sense enough to avoid that. He put on his hat and raincoat, pulling his hat a little more than usual over one eye. His picked up his bag and was about to leave when, with a grunt of alarm, he remembered the waste-paper basket. He went across and stared down in cold anger and frustration at the stained cotton-wool. There was too much to carry in his pockets and these hotels provided you with everything except a fireplace. He picked up a piece of the wool and carried it over to the wash-basin, but in time his common sense warned him that it would take too long to burn there and would fill the room with smoke. At last he opened his case and stuffed the wool down on top of the notepaper. This time he was really off.

Downstairs he paid his bill and got into the waiting taxi. The commissionaire, expecting his tip, hovered round the door and so had to hear him say 'King's Cross'. Not that it mattered. Who'd be likely to remember so commonplace a destination?

In the taxi he leaned back and realized he might have been running. Fool again. Nerves. He lit a cigarette. That was better. Not really a nervous man. It would pass in a day or two. What a weight she'd been, dragging to the bed; her shoe had caught in the carpet. He'd dream of that. But his coolness then had paid. Run, he'd thought, run; all that noise; but instead he'd listened and held firm. That had taken courage. Cold courage. Some day he'd be proud of that.

And then the meeting at the foot of the stairs . . .

Half-way to the station he saw a paper-man on a corner and spoke through to the driver. While out he posted one of the letters and then sat back, opening out the newspaper in haste.

Oh, it was there now; there in splashed headlines as he'd expected.

But not quite the headlines he'd expected. There was an unexpected complication.

Hurriedly his eyes skipped through the account, puzzled, only half believing. It seemed like a trap. Carefully he went through it again, studying every word, his blood throbbing in his head. It wasn't until he finished it for a third time that he felt fully assured that this might really for him be the easy way out.

Chapter Eight

THAT NIGHT *Rigoletto* went off in very good style.

The next night came *Traviata*, with Philippa in the leading role, and the Opera House was besieged. The high praise of her singing on the Monday, together with two days of intense publicity over her husband's detention at Bow Street, had fired the town's curiosity. Suave men in evening dress hurried sweating about the Opera House, afraid of a riot.

Twenty minutes late and in this curious air of notoriety, the curtain went up, and Philippa played and sang the story of La Dame aux Camélias, with no kind husband to support her, but only her own courage and her iron determination not to let the company down. The evening was another personal triumph; but when it was all over she had only the strength to tell Marie to keep everyone out of her dressing-room, and it was midnight before she recovered the stamina to go home.

Even then there were a half-dozen reporters and a curious crowd at the stage door. Flashlights hissed and flared and men tried to get in her way. 'Miss Shelley, may we have a short statement,' and 'Miss Shelley, what is your opinion of . . .' and 'Can you help us, Miss Shelley; your plans . . .' Then the taxi door was slammed by the door-keeper, and she was alone and safe again.

But safe only until the morning; for in the morning, soon after ten o'clock, Nicolas James Talbot was to be brought up in Bow Street Police Court. Although she knew nothing of the law and Mr Frobisher was trying to keep her in ignorance of it, she felt that their refusal to

66

allow Nick bail and this quick move to bring him into court were very bad signs indeed.

And so it proved. In the small, sour, unimpressive court-room the evidence for the police was mustered. In spite of herself she had to admit that this evidence, though all circumstantial, seemed to fit together and was full of substance. She knew that the police would never have moved if they hadn't been fairly sure of their ground. Now and then she looked at Nick and at Frobisher and at the '*Dieu et mon droit*' behind the magistrate's head; but for the most part she kept her eyes down to avoid the stares of the crowded court, whose curiosity seemed equally divided between her and the man in the dock. It went on and on, and then to her surprise the magistrate suddenly remanded Nick in custody until tomorrow when the hearing would be resumed.

As the court emptied, John and Joan Newcombe came across to her, and John, a middle-aged stockbroker with a matter-of-fact manner, said:

'Come along, my dear. We're going to look after you today.'

'Oh, no,' she said. 'Please don't bother, either of you. I don't want to give you any trouble, and I'll be all right. Really I will.'

'We'll go and have a meal somewhere,' Joan said. 'I know you can't eat a thing,' she added, meeting Philippa's objection before she made it, 'but it will do you good just the same.'

Without the will to resist further, Philippa left the court with them, and then was glad of their car as a means of avoiding the curious crowd outside.

With warm food steaming before her, she realized she had had no breakfast that morning and very little of anything the day before. Slowly she began to eat.

67

Joan said: 'You must spend tonight with us. I couldn't think of your going back to that solitary flat. Then John will drive you up again in the morning.'

'You're very kind,' said Philippa. She suddenly found her eyes full of tears and blinked them away.

'Well, he's my brother,' said Joan. 'Why shouldn't we be?'

Philippa said: 'Well, you see ... you hardly know me, and I thought perhaps the way this had happened ... It was my fault, wasn't it? Throwing that thing ... and ...'

'Nonsense,' said Joan. 'I feel it's the sort of awful thing that might have happened to anyone.'

John sat reflective for a moment. 'Are you thinking of that time at Cannes?' he asked her.

'Well, I wasn't thinking specially of ourselves. *Mightn't* it have happened to almost anyone? But now you mention it...'

John said: 'Two years after we were married, Philippa, we went to Cannes for a holiday, one of those rather vulgar holidays when one goes everywhere and does everything; and one night we were invited to a private dance by a man we had met there. During the evening Joan flirted outrageously with a little dago from South America or somewhere—'

'A pure-bred Spaniard,' Joan said.

'—and we had words, and I said if she felt like that I was going to leave her to it, and I said good night and went out to the car, and Joan came after me, feeling furious and humiliated, as she's told me since. Then in the car we had more words, and somehow before we realized it I'd slapped her face, and she'd scratched me with her nails: two long scratches from my left eyebrow; I fancy I can see the marks today.'

'Fortunately it's only fancy,' Joan said, 'but I never felt

so awful in my life as when I saw what I'd done. It wasn't quite intentional even at the time – and yet . . .'

'I know,' said Philippa.

'That was fourteen years ago. But you'll see that even stockbrokers have their moments.'

'And stockbrokers' wives,' said Joan.

They talked on, about ordinary mundane things, and for a time the enormity of the present dilemma came to stand among the other events of life and not seem disproportionate. In the end Philippa agreed gratefully to spend the night with them in Surrey. It was a great relief to her to have some sane and friendly companionship after the strain of the last three days, but she stipulated that her visit should be for one night only, for somehow she could not be comfortable so far from the centre of things at this time. And there was a rehearsal late tomorrow afternoon.

Despite the quiet and the comfort she slept badly, thinking of Nick, and was glad enough when it was time to leave. They drove up to Town, and it seemed in no time at all they were back in the stuffy, crowded police court and Nick was in the dock again looking neat and composed, and the evidence against him was slowly piling up. The morning wore on, and presently Mr Frobisher got up to make one of his brief – his all too brief – statements. Then, with a growing sensation of sick horror, she heard the magistrate's voice committing Nicolas James Talbot to stand his trial at the Old Bailey on a charge of the wilful murder of Elizabeth Rusman.

The hearing was finished, and for a moment she could not move. People were filing past her; the Newcombes had risen and were coming towards her; Mr Frobisher turned and asked her something; through a haze she saw Inspector Archer moving bulkily and neatly off.

She got up quickly and pushed past somebody and reached him as he was about to leave.

'*Could* I have a word with you, Inspector?'

'Certainly, Mrs Talbot.'

'Alone, I mean.'

Archer exchanged a glance and a few words with his companion and led the way across the yard from the court to the police station, and then up the linoleum-covered stairs to a small office furnished like a provincial bank manager's with two or three group photographs on the walls.

'Inspector Archer,' she said, getting the words out before they failed her, 'I beg of you, how long is this farce going on?'

He fingered the documents he carried, and for a moment his eyes went over the first few words. '*Rex* v. *Talbot, Nicolas James. Offence: Offences Against the Person Act, 1861. Murder. Copy. Depositions of Proceedings Before Court of Summary Jurisdiction.*

He said: 'I'm afraid we don't look on it in that light.'

'What we've heard this morning,' she said. 'The same evidence . . . what does it amount to?'

'Circumstantially, a very strong case, I'm afraid.'

'So you don't believe what I have said about our quarrel?'

Archer shifted uncomfortably. These personal interviews were always trying; they would become intolerable on this level.

'It's not for me to believe or disbelieve, Mrs Talbot. I'm a servant of the Crown, and really this case is out of my hands now. I collect the evidence, but other people decide whether that evidence is strong enough for the case to proceed to trial. Personally, and for your sake, I'm very sorry . . . But it's only fair to remind you that you and your

70

husband told conflicting stories to begin. And even if there was this quarrel—'

'Even!'

'—you must realize that the case for the Crown would not therefore fall through. On your own admission as to times, there was ample time for your husband to walk round to Elizabeth Rusman's flat *afterwards* and commit the murder. Your alibi is really no alibi at all, as the evidence given today amply shows.'

She was silent then, staring out at the cloudy spring sky. His eyes went over her. She was wearing a little black hat today with a half veil which, by cloaking the upper half of her face, made her warm sensitive mouth more attractive than ever. Not like a singer somehow, he thought. Too slender; they usually ran to fat. Great breasts on them. Or was that an outdated idea? The papers had made a fuss about her. Evidently she was going to be one of the big noises. They were making a fuss about this case too. He could see the headlines today: '*Ex-Guards Officer Committed for Trial*', '*Husband of Opera Star for Old Bailey*'. Flogging all the conventional horses to keep the public's interest sharp. Oh, well, he supposed the publicity would do her no harm. At least she must be given the credit for seeming to hate it. Hadn't given a single interview so far. She was very much in love with this chap, one could see that. She would lie her eyes away to save him.

Philippa said: 'The Crown has quite made up its mind it has caught the murderer?'

He blew some air out of his cheeks. 'The Crown thinks it has a good case. Twelve ordinary citizens will decide whether it's good enough.'

She turned from the window. 'Can you try just for a minute to see it as I see it. I *know* you're mistaken. I *know*

Nick couldn't have done it. Then don't you see how I must feel, knowing that there must be a real murderer and knowing that he's having all this time to put himself farther and farther out of your reach?'

'Let me reassure you that intensive inquiries are still going on.'

'How much do you know about Elizabeth Rusman?' she asked. 'Surely more than was told in court?'

'Well, strictly speaking, Mrs Talbot, I don't know that I'm in order giving you these details; but in the circumstances . . . We know that she was thirty-one and born in London. Her father, a Dutchman, was a naturalized British citizen and represented a Dutch steamship company. He was in Rotterdam at the time of the 1940 German raid, and was killed there. Her mother was English and died young. Elizabeth was an only child and early broke away and earned her living playing in small orchestras. In 1942 she went to America in charge of some Dutch children. She stayed with the family until last year, and seems to have come back to this country a month or two ago, though she must have travelled under an assumed name, since there is no record of it. Her first traceable appearance in this country was four weeks ago, when she called on her old agents, Messrs Till and Barrett, and asked them to find her employment.' Archer laid down his notes.

'When did she leave this family in America?' Philippa asked.

'About nine months ago, we're told.'

'So that she may actually have been back in England nearly nine months?'

Archer shook his head. 'Nine months ago it was almost impossible for a private citizen to travel. Even today she must have been fairly ingenious to get a passage.'

'But she may have made all sorts of contacts while she was in America. She may have been with half a dozen men since Nick.'

'Indeed she may,' Archer conceded. 'The medical evidence shows that at some time she has had a child. But her character with the Dutch family in America was quite exemplary.'

'Why did she leave them?' Philippa asked.

'Their children were growing up and they no longer needed her.'

Philippa turned from the window. She knew that this big tidy man was waiting for her to go.

'I suppose you've – circulated a photograph and done everything possible?'

'Up to now we haven't been able to lay our hands on one. A description, of course.'

'Well, she shouldn't be hard to describe. I only saw her once . . .'

Archer said: 'Unfortunately the fire, you know. She wasn't . . .'

Philippa made a grimace. 'That may make it more difficult.'

'A little, perhaps.'

'Well, thank you, Inspector. You've been very patient with me.'

From the station Philippa went straight across to the Opera House. The Newcombes had gone, and although there were a number of people about she was lucky enough to slip across without being recognized. She went straight through to Ravogli's office, knowing he would be there at this time of the morning.

Aware of the opposition she would face, she plunged straight into her decision, and for three minutes Giuseppi

Ravogli sat unspeaking behind his big desk watching her with his soulful but astute brown eyes. Then, like a time-bomb which has reached the end of its fuse, he blew up into passionate Italian. For five minutes they argued in a mixture of languages, Ravogli gradually coming round to speak English, as she refused to be moved either from that or from her decision.

'Do you mean it!' he exclaimed, tears of self-pity in his voice. 'I cannot believe it! The husband. Yes, that I under-stand. But what has the husband to do with art? Profession is a thing separated. What is it about? You destroy me!'

Philippa said: 'Singing means so much and this chance is so terrific that nothing less than life and death would make me fall out. *You* know that. You know I've never let you or Arturo down before. But I can't go on like last night now that Nick's committed for trial. It's not humanly possible. I *can't* go on. If you can't get a substitute for tomorrow I'll sing then, but not afterwards.'

'Substitute! Who is to substitute? Don't make me severe. What have you to please me? There is no one!'

'Try Angelina. She's wasted as Suzuki. She deserves her chance.'

'A mezzo! Not yet twenty!'

'With a lovely fresh voice. She could do it, I'm sure.'

Giuseppi tapped the desk. 'Look. I patronize you! I produce you! You are here! A sensation! The English for once can appreciate the English. *Contento*; I am happy. And what? Is it possible? She has lost herself. I know, I know, *I know*. It is not your mistake. You would avert this, will you tell me. But how we must all suffer for the error of this one. Oh, why do you ruin yourself with marriage!' The producer's English gave out again.

'You could wire for Frenetti,' said Philippa.

'Frenetti! Nothing! *Mi sento male.*'

She got up and went round the desk. 'Forgive me, Giuseppi. Don't you see how much I feel this myself? Dear Giuseppi, please understand. I am so unhappy. So miserable. You know Nick. How can I desert him? How *could* I go on?'

'But how do you help him by going off?'

'I don't know yet. I've got to think. There must be some way. It's like a heavy cloud over us all. I must feel absolutely free to go anywhere. It wouldn't be fair to you to try to sing. It's exacting. You know how exacting. In the end I should let you down. I'm sure of it. They say the trial will come on soon after Easter. Until then I can only possibly have one thing on my mind, and it won't be music. Perhaps there are things I can do that the police can't. At least I'll try.'

'And I,' said Giuseppi, 'am left in a ditch!'

'I'm so very sorry. But you can get someone else. Angelina is on the spot. Maria would do it as well as her present work. Or you can get someone new from Europe. Only give me a month from the time I go off. Even then if – if all goes well there will be still two weeks of the season left.'

He took out a large handkerchief and wiped his eyes. 'You are hard in the heart, Philippa. I can do nothing with you. I am sorry for it. You will play tomorrow?'

'If you can't make any different arrangement.'

'Have the goodness to know that I cannot. But think over it. Think over this chance for your life which may not come back again any more. Think over, dear girl. And don't imagine I forgive you! I am hurt!'

Philippa took a taxi back to the flat. Hurt, hurt, that was Giuseppi's last word. And it was the keynote of all these past days.

It hurt to take this step which could permanently blight her career. Until a few days ago she would have said her singing meant more to her than anything in life. It meant all the more because she had had no royal road to it. She had sold the railway stock her mother left her at slump prices to scrape enough money together to go to Italy. Often in those first years of study she had gone hungry and cold. Now that success had come to her while she was still in the early twenties she was eagerly anxious to grasp it, to build it up by quick repetition while it was still there. The striving, the climbing, were still too near to be comfortable.

Yet now she threw up this wonderful opportunity of endearing herself to the London opera-going public almost without hesitation and knowing that Nick would be as angry as anyone. She did not even know how she would come through on Saturday evening. It was as if anxiety was holding her throat.

As the taxi turned into the street where her flat was she saw two men idling outside the door. She quickly told the driver to go round to the back where there was another entrance. She remembered once in Naples seeing a well-known actor dunned by creditors. He had done just the same as she did now.

The flat when she entered was dull and lifeless. Mrs Saunders did not come on Fridays, and the place had a neglected dusty air. She went through to the jade-green bathroom, peered earnestly at herself for a moment and then rinsed her throat with some stuff prescribed by a Paris doctor. Then she stood at a window doing breathing exercises, ruthlessly pushing out of her mind the horrors of the police-court hearing. Described as it had been described, the case against Nick *did* look bad. Why deny it? Obviously the magistrate could not dismiss the case and set Nick free. Unless another man was found, the charge had to be thrashed out in the full light of a legal trial.

She finished her exercises, realizing that she had begun them by thrusting away from her all thoughts of Nick's plight, and almost at once they had come creeping in again, like herself, by the back door.

She went to the window and saw that the reporters had not gone away. They were waiting for her. Well, very soon they would know she was in. She went to the piano and began to run her fingers up and down the keys. The light from the window fell on her long fair hair. Then she began to sing her scales, rather softly at first.

Normally it was an exercise which soothed her; voice and nerves always benefited by it; there was something in the regularity, the easy long-accustomed rhythms, that calmed and refreshed her throat. Even today, in spite of everything, she began to feel easier, more confident, as she went on. Somehow these weeks would pass, this nightmare would pass. With a month's complete freedom she could do so much. Long before then everything might be cleared up, such new facts might be brought to light that the trial would be abandoned. Things would straighten themselves out. Innocent men weren't condemned. It was just a bad time to be passed through.

The front-door bell rang.

She took no notice, going through the next scale and the next, her voice soaring effortlessly, with her spirits, like the wind.

The front-door bell rang again. She stopped and went to the window. One of the reporters had disappeared. He was evidently inside. She went back to the piano.

For a time she went on with her singing, and for a time the reporter persisted with the bell. Then he gave up, and presently, her concentration gone, she gave up too. The silence in the flat suddenly became profound.

Nothing stirred, no board creaked or kettle boiled. No friendly voice or familiar footsteps disturbed the lonely day.

Philippa leaned forward on the piano and laid her head on her arms.

Chapter Nine

FOUR HUNDRED AND NINE railway miles away, Mr Sidney Fleming was reading the London papers which had just come.

From where he was sitting he could hear C Form at their chanting, and he wondered if Mr Duncan was in one of his moods. (Duncan with his thin greying hair, his sour breath, his jealousies, his dreary Latin jokes. It was hopeless to make all the changes one could have wished with the present council of governors.)

The school clock chimed two-thirty and he folded the papers on his desk. Some Thursdays he took an extra class in the afternoons, but today he was free until four. He put on his gown and mortar-board and went out. All the classrooms were full and he met nobody, walking, a well-proportioned but unathletic figure, through the grounds of the school, past the porter's lodge and out upon the main road that ran down the hill to the village. A bone-chilling wind was blowing in from the sea.

He stopped at a grey slate house built on a corner and turning its sash windows towards the land for shelter. Asked inside, he stood a few minutes in the waiting-room, his hands behind his back, his meditative eyes fixed on the wall; then he turned to shake hands with the physician, a hearty man in the fifties.

'Mr Fleming, I was hoping it was a social call you were paying us. I don't look for you in my consulting-room, man.'

'I'm not expecting to trouble you a great deal, Dr Wishart. But I've been sleeping badly these last weeks, and

79

thought you might have some patent dose of your own which would help to compose me. It wears one down after a time.'

'Aye.' Wishart gave the other a professional glance. 'Lack of sleep's worse than lack of food, you know. D'you get any pain?'

'Oh, I don't think there is anything organically wrong. But naturally during term-time one can't afford to be below par.'

Dr Wishart made a few tests. 'Your heart's a bit excitable. I should cut down smoking. Apart from that ... Maybe you're over-working, then can't relax. Any worries?'

'Nothing out of the common. You've kept us uncommonly free from epidemics this year.'

Wishart smiled, and his eyes scanned the other man's face. A face full of character, full of contradictions, the long smooth cheeks, the intent eyes of an idealist, the tight uncompromising mouth: one had no farther to look for conflict than in the man himself. You could imagine him writing mystic poetry or thrashing small children; four hundred years ago he would have been a Protestant martyr or perhaps writing tracts *against* the Reformation. One sensed there was religion in him, but it was religion in revolt.

'I'll make you up a bottle and some tablets.'

The doctor went into his dispensary, and while he was gone Fleming turned again to his gazing at the featureless wall.

'Take this three times a day and a tablet before you go to bed. By the by, I heard from your wife yesterday.'

Fleming watched him. 'Indeed?'

'You know I attended her privately around Christmas –

for nerves. She seems worried that she hasn't settled this account and asks me to send it in to you. It is quite needlessly kind of her to take the trouble and I must write and reassure her that we were suffering no qualms—'

'I will save you further trouble by reassuring her on the point. But let me have both accounts some time, there's a good fellow.'

Wishart said: 'She's not coming back yet, then? I hope she's better.'

'I doubt if she'll be back this term. Her friends want her to stay, and the change suits her. She finds it over-quiet up here.'

'Yes? Well, it's what you get accustomed to, no doubt. Come in and see us some evening, if you've the mind. There's much we can talk of. Friday's my best day.'

'Thank you,' said Fleming, satisfied. 'Good-bye.'

At high tea Mrs Wishart said: 'Was that Mr Fleming I saw this afternoon? Nothing wrong at the school, I hope?'

'No,' said her husband. 'He came for a tonic for himself.'

Mrs Wishart stirred her tea. 'Well, I've no doubt he needs it with all they boys to be concerned about. But I hadn't thought of him as an ailing man. Eat your tea, David.'

Wishart put down his paper. 'These kippers are a wee bit salt for my personal taste. Did you get them from MacAndrew?'

'Aye. Did he say when Mrs Fleming would be coming back?'

'Fleming? Maybe not this term, he said.'

Mrs Wishart buttered a piece of toast and passed the butter to her husband. 'It's no more than what I expected. I doubt she'll ever come back to him.'

'What makes you say that?'

'Well, you know as well as I do that they were often on bad terms.'

'Oh, yes, but . . . that was just the way things are sometimes. You've been listening to the gossips, Janet.'

'Well, they were hammer and tongs at the end of the Christmas term. Mrs Bunce told Maggie that. Then in the middle of term she goes away to relatives in London. But when she should come back she doesn't come back, an' last week-end he goes travelling off to London, leaving Mr Grant in charge. I've no doubt that's why he's in need of a tonic if they've come to a break, for he's a right-thinking man and wouldn't take it lightly.'

Dr Wishart eyed his wife a moment. 'Drummond told me yesterday that Lady Clunes said Fleming was in the running for Lovell's at Glasgow. But it won't improve his chances if he's separated from his wife.'

'Och, I don't think *she* would have improved his chances anyhow. She never was the type for a headmaster's wife. Too fond of criss-crossing her legs on the platform on prize-giving days.'

Wishart pulled some bones out of his mouth and grunted in mild amusement.

'Well, I daresay there were faults on both sides – he wouldn't be an easy man to live with – but I don't like to hear of a marriage broken up for such inadequate reasons.'

'David, what *was* the matter with her when she came to see you in January?'

Wishart grunted again. 'Nerves and a few bruises.'

'Bruises?' said Janet Wishart. 'You mean—'

'I don't mean anything. It's not my business to mean anything, my dear. No doubt she got them doing her own housework.'

'Inadequate reasons!' said Mrs Wishart. 'I'd no idea he was a man like that. I've a mind not to ask him here again!'

'I've heard from that Mrs Fleming,' said Mrs Mac-Ardle. 'She'll not be needing our upstairs room again.' She lifted the ring off the stove and poked the fire. A cloud of dust arose. 'This coal.'

'Turn up the draught,' said Mr MacArdle, moving his wheel-chair nearer the window. 'You know it always makes me cough.'

'She says she's leaving the district and going to live on the Clyde. Now that's imagination, for the dust rose straight up. Anyone would think I blacked my kitchen on purpose to aggravate you.'

Mr MacArdle's cough died away. 'Why anyone should go to live near Glasgow after living in Edinboro' is a pretty problem. What did she come here for, anyway? Who should pay good money to hire a room for the sake of playing on a violin once or twice a month? Did she not have her ain house?'

'Her husband disliked the sound of it, she said, and I'm not all that surprised, knowing the noises she made here from time to time. It was a whim, I imagine, and now she's tired of it.' Mrs MacArdle put on the potatoes to boil. Not until she heard a comfortable *bubble-bubble* from inside the pan did she release her firm grip of the handle.

Mr MacArdle's good right hand had been tugging at his tobacco pouch. He grunted his satisfaction as it came out, and he began to fill his pipe. He spilled shreds of tobacco on the floor.

'The papers are making a rare fuss about this woman violinist who's been murdered,' he said. 'I haven't seen a photo yet.'

Mrs MacArdle said tartly: 'Well, as she was killed last Monday and this letter was posted in Glasgie yesterday, it's not likely to be our Mrs Fleming now, is it? Besides, that woman was a *professional*. . . .'

Chapter Ten

PHILIPPA WENT TO Queen's Bench Chambers to meet
Mr Stephen Tyler, K.C., who was looked on as a rising
young man at the Bar. The fact that he was forty-four and
nearly bald did not affect the issue in a profession where
wigs are still worn and talent matures late. He had taken
silk six months ago, after only eight years as a successful
junior – and that separated from the post-war world by a
long spell of military service – but the risk had already
been justified.

With so much at stake Philippa would really have preferred an older and more experienced man, but Frobisher,
grey and cautious enough himself, had scented out Tyler
as the one man for whom this case seemed ideally suited;
so to Tyler they came.

He greeted her with just the right amount of deference
due to her as a beautiful woman, saw her in friendly
fashion to a chair, resumed his own seat in some dignity
and picked up the brief which he had read through for the
first time an hour before.

They discussed it at some length, he treading delicately with his questions and comments, sizing up
Philippa's attitude, careful to seek out the salient points
of the prosecution, like a new general searching for his
enemy's big guns, probing also into the lines he would
have to defend, making himself aware of the weakness and
the inconsistencies.

He did not ask too many questions at this first meeting
for fear of upsetting her uncertain composure and for fear
of appearing dubious of the result. But he got most of the

information he wanted. He nodded slow approval of Frobisher's attitude at the police court, though privately he always had mental reservations on a policy of altogether withholding one's defence (there was the opinion of the general public to consider, from among whom twelve good men had necessarily to be chosen; and leaving a case unanswered before the magistrate meant leaving the prosecution with a clear field during the formative weeks).

'Well, it's an interesting case, Mr Frobisher,' he said eventually. 'Mrs Talbot was fortunate to have a friend in you. I should like to study this further in the course of the week.' He flipped the brief, and his handsome prominent eyes met Philippa's. 'Don't allow yourself to be worried in this matter, Mrs Talbot,' he said positively. 'As baldly stated, the case has its unfavourable aspects. But there are several very promising factors which haven't yet been given their full weight. There's a great deal to be done with it. That's always an encouraging sign. It's the case which seems to offer no scope for treatment that is the bugbear of counsel.'

'You'll accept the brief?' Philippa asked, anxious to be quite clear.

'Emphatically. I can already see one clear line of defence. But a great deal of preliminary detail remains to be clarified at present. It will give me very great personal satisfaction if I can help in preventing what would be a grave miscarriage of justice. I'll call you tomorrow, Mr Frobisher. We must make arrangements for visiting Captain Talbot.'

Philippa left the chambers feeling comforted. Apart from friends and some of Nick's relatives, like the Newcombes, the K.C. was the first man who had spoken so hopefully of the outcome. The cautious Frobisher and his partner had never committed themselves to definite statements of opinion. Discreetly and competently they had gone about their business and left speculation to others. Without meaning to, they had undermined her confidence. Tyler had handed it back to her with a determined gesture of his long white hands. She felt that both she and Nick had found a friend who really believed in his innocence and would make others think the same. Frobisher did not tell her that the barrister's peculiarly mobile, impetuous sympathy gave this impression to most of his clients.

When they had gone Tyler stalked across to the office on the other side of the passage where his devil, Arthur McNeill, was poring over some papers. McNeill looked up as a bundle of fresh papers was dropped on the table before him. Tyler did not speak but went and stood with his back to the fire, his brilliant eyes fixed on his colleague.

There was silence.

'A fortnight's work for you, Arthur. Drop that other stuff and put your mind to this. This Talbot fellow, who's accused of strangling his mistress. It's all before you.'

'You're leading?' McNeill said, screwing up his face as he stared at the top page. 'What's the odds?'

'Heavy against him, but it's all circumstantial. We can shake that. There are things in his favour, obvious things: his education, his army career, his good reputation—'

'I shouldn't bank too much on that, Stephen.'

Tyler flung up his arm. 'Rot. We can get an acquittal. There's one definite line. But I want your opinion. Go through it piece by piece. If you have any idea come and tell me. The man's innocent, I feel, and it will be a good life to save.'

On Good Friday Philippa paid one of her usual visits to Nick, who had been moved to Brixton Remand Prison.

It took quite a lot to frighten Philippa, but this place

did. From the outside it might have been a medieval castle built by some gloomy baron whose rule rested on terror and brute power. But inside it was much, much worse. As far as she could see it consisted – apart from the endless disinfected stone corridors and the blank lime-washed reception-rooms – of a number of great chambers with the cells in tiers, looking across at each other from among barred balustrades and iron ladders. Such things she had seen in American prison films but had never before quite believed in. Nick called them the Mappin Terraces.

But privately his sense of humour was wearing a little thin. While he was in Bow Street he had not quite been able to take the charge seriously; although he had hated it all he had not in his heart believed the police meant to bring him up on a capital charge. It was his move to Brixton, far more than the magistrates' committal, which had brought it home to the very last detail. The English law said he was innocent until proved guilty; but in the interim police law inevitably had to ensure that he was maintained, guarded, fed, regimented and preserved until such time as he came up for trial. He was treated kindly enough, allowed to keep his own clothes, to smoke and to read in off times and was allowed to see Philippa once a day. But he had been stripped, searched, medically examined, deprived of all articles which might tempt him to suicide and locked away in a cell. Each day he was exercised with other prisoners awaiting trial; each day the prison ate away his good spirits: the high draughty glooms of the place, the noises of clanking buckets and nailed boots, the hygienic but unsavoury smells. If he had been guilty he felt he would long since have lost all hope. It seemed even to implant a sense of guilt where none existed. Sometimes he woke in the night and began to sweat at his thoughts.

To Philippa he was always bright enough, but she

knew him well enough to see beneath the surface. Perhaps she even read into his mind some of her own feelings At Bow Street he had said he didn't suffer from claustrophobia, but she felt that no one could fail to suffer from it in this place. Her own imprisonment in Italy had been in fairly pleasant surroundings and with plenty of latitude inside the camp, but even there the endless years had weighed so heavy on her that at times she had felt herself inside a tiny contracting cage against which she must beat her fists and cry out. How much worse must Nick feel inside what was *in fact* a tiny cage, knowing what was before him and knowing that all the time the law was working to get him more securely in its grip.

Sometimes, to deflect her obvious distress, he joined in her attempts at amateur detection, though he hadn't the slightest faith in them. He could see that her activity was useful to her if not to him. On only one point did he argue angrily with her, and that was on the breaking of her operatic career. He felt that her withdrawing at this stage would do him no good and herself untold harm. He was set on her becoming the leading European soprano of the day, and confident that nothing much stood in her way. He could fend for himself. In any case, irrespective of his own future, they must think of hers.

After two weeks of freedom Philippa was tired but not discouraged, and she was anxious to tell him her movements and her plans. She had been making inquiries, treading uselessly in the footsteps of the police. Wherever she went they had been first; but there was a consolation in this active response to Nick's imprisonment. Not only did it help to salve her conscience over that night, it also occupied her mind and body in the only way it was at present willing to work.

She had been to Elizabeth Rusman's lodgings, but had

been turned away; she had met Mike Grieve and talked with him, but his response had been surly. Some of the lodgers were more agreeable, but their information hadn't helped, since they were out at the time of the murder. Later she had called on Mr Till, who had found Elizabeth Rusman her new engagement, and he had been very helpful in giving her the history of Elizabeth Rusman's pre-war employments. This had given her something to work on, and she had been all over the south of England.

Yet every alley was blind after a few turns, and every contact she made was curiously lacking in another respect. Nowhere could she find a friend of Elizabeth Rusman. Acquaintances enough, and one or two people who had known her pretty well, but none would agree to the description as applied to themselves. 'Well,' they would say, 'I knew her quite well and for a time we went about a bit together, but I wouldn't say we were exactly *friends*.' It seemed that when she came back to England after her long absence she had looked up none of these acquaintances she had made before. Philippa wondered why.

Of course there was much to be done yet – especially in America. But as she went about her quest this week she realized that through a mistaken sense of not wanting to re-open a subject which had been the cause of their quarrel she was neglecting a source which might supply the answer to that question and a number of others as well. There was one person who could not deny he had known Elizabeth intimately, and that was . . .

'Nick,' she said, breaking in at the end of something he was saying, 'I want you to tell me more about Elizabeth Rusman.'

He frowned, changing the direction of his thoughts; looked at her over the glass partition that was between them and lifted one eyebrow in quizzical concern.

'Haven't we had enough of her?'

'No. Not nearly enough, Nick. Since that awful night we've avoided her like the plague—'

'I thought we'd done nothing else but talk of her.'

'Oh, yes, of the murder. But not of what happened five years ago. I want to know all about that. It may give me some idea of why she acted as she did, going off to America—'

'I've told the police all the facts.'

'All they've asked. But not the whole history of it, where you met, what happened ... Forget I was ever jealous, Nick. This is – above pettiness. Remember that she's dead and you're accused of killing her. You're in danger, terrible danger. No sort of false shyness must stand in our way over this. I want to know—'

'What good will knowing it do you?'

'I can't tell. I don't know till I hear. But I want to hear.'

He shrugged. 'Some time perhaps—'

'No. Now.'

He was silent. 'Oh, it's nonsense.'

'Tell me, please,' she said. 'Tell me how you first met.'

He lit a cigarette, glanced at his watch.

'It was after I came back from Nigeria – you know, I'd been prospecting for the government out there. I'd come back to join up and met her at a house-party. We – more or less teamed up at once. I got very fond of her and in fact toyed with the idea of marriage; it was then that I wrote those letters the police found, but somehow it didn't really get round to marriage. We quarrelled and separated and came together again, and quite suddenly, without any special cause except the war, decided to go off together. We spent three weeks in Wales. Then we quarrelled again and that was the end of it. I was drafted abroad almost at once and never saw her again until the night at Covent Garden.'

He met his wife's gaze. His eyes were embarrassed but a little relieved, as if he was thankful that much was over.

'But why did you quarrel?' she asked.

He looked at his cigarette. 'I don't know.'

'You must know.'

'Damn it!' He knocked the ask off into a tray. 'What does one quarrel about? The simplest, absurdest things. We should know.'

'But you weren't going to leave me, were you?'

'Of course not. You silly. That was quite different. Very soon after we went away I realized I didn't really love her. It made the last part of our three weeks a dismal failure. When—'

'But what made you decide you didn't love her?'

He shook his head as if trying to shake away the question. 'I don't know, Philippa. She was pretty, she was fun; but it was one of those things. Intimacy is a sort of crucible, I think: either it refines one's love or the feeling disintegrates and proves to be fake. My feeling was fake. That was why I had rather a guilty conscience about her when we met again back stage.'

'Why?'

'Well, I *had* been fond of her, and I did leave her. And the interval of years had rather glossed over her fault and made me feel a heel about it.'

There was silence. Time was nearly up.

Philippa said: 'Do you think she went with other men?'

'I wasn't the first. But she was not the sort who would go off with anybody for the sake of a good time. She would have married me if it had got that far.'

'Did she never speak to you of her friends?'

'I don't think so.'

'Or her plans?'

'I can't remember that she did. Anyway, it's surely so long ago that it can hardly have any bearing.'

'You can never be sure, Nick. Think. Try to think. Anything. Your life may depend on it.'

'Don't you think I'd help you if I possibly could?'

'Tomorrow I'm going to Holland to see her only living aunt. She may have visited her there since the liberation. While I'm away think hard of everything you did together, any names she may have mentioned, anything which could help me.'

'I'd far rather think of the time I've spent with you.'

'I've also been trying to get an air passage to America,' she said. 'They say they're all booked, but perhaps I can get some sort of priority. It seems almost certain now that the clue lies in New York.'

The prison officer sitting at the end of their table gave a discreet cough. It was borne in upon Nick that because of her going to Holland he would not see her for two or three days. The shadow of this knowledge crossed his eyes. Her visit was the only thing in the day.

'Don't worry,' he said. 'I like the looks of Tyler. I'm sure it will be all right.'

'Between us we'll make it sure,' she said, and turned to go.

Chapter Eleven

PHILIPPA THOUGHT OF her promise several times during the Easter week-end she spent at The Hague. Tyler, like herself, would do his best; but she hoped his efforts would be surer than hers. In a little scrupulously tidy kitchen she saw the old aunt, while a cat rubbed against her legs and fitful sun lit up the patterns of the faded rugs.

Through an interpreter it was almost impossible to get at the surviving Miss Rusman. She was worse than deaf, being inattentive with the mental deafness of old age. Once her mind had been edged into the right groove it went clicking over into the well-worn ridges of opinion formed twenty years ago. Even Philippa, who knew no word of the language, could pick out the repetitions. Elizabeth had always been a wilful child; no care for her parents. No, she had not seen her for many years. She was not the sort of girl to come visiting her old relatives. No, she had no photograph, except one at the age of five with her father, which the police had taken. What? Oh, yes, the police had been. She was not surprised, for Elizabeth had always been a wilful child, no care for her parents. Other relatives? Yes, there was one; Peter Schuyleman, who lived at Utrecht. A cousin. Age? About the same age as Elizabeth, who had always been a wilful child. . . .

On Sunday Philippa went to Utrecht and found that Peter Schuyleman had died during the occupation. On the Monday she returned to England and the following morning early she called again on Inspector Archer and told him she had decided to go to America – could he furnish her with the necessary addresses.

Archer looked at her with a certain degree of discomfort. He noted the signs of fatigue on the girl's face.

'It's less than ten days to the trial, Mrs Talbot,' he said. 'You could do nothing in the time. All that side has been covered, I assure you.'

'It's better than – just sitting waiting. I might find out something. I'd rather go.'

He said: 'You've been tiring yourself out enough, Mrs Talbot.'

'Oh, it isn't what I've been doing,' she said, 'so much as knowing that my husband's innocent – it's the knowing that you're making a terrible mistake and not being able to do anything to stop it.'

He had been watching her very closely. He was not a mean judge of character.

She said: 'Can you give me permission to see the room where the murder took place? They wouldn't let me in.'

'We can do that. But the room has been cleaned up and everything taken out.'

'And Elizabeth Rusman's belongings?'

'Some of them are exhibits at the trial.'

'But not all. Not everything she wore and . . .'

'I can show you some of the things. Isn't it rather a forlorn hope?'

'It's almost a last hope. But sometimes a woman notices things . . .'

He picked up a telephone and spoke into it. After a few minutes a constable brought in a suitcase and a violin case. He put them on a table, unlocked them and then withdrew. Slowly Philippa rose and went over to the table. She lifted the lid of the suitcase and stared down at the clothes within, some of them charred and almost ready to crumble. As she touched them there rose to her nostrils a faint feminine scent. It was the only remaining trace of the personality of their owner. Philippa shivered.

Archer had come to stand beside her. She forced herself to go on lifting them out.

'Is there nothing in these things to give you any clue at all?' she asked.

'The suit is from Paris Modes, who have shops all over the country. The shoes are from multiple shops. The nightdress is Celanese. The evening dress was bought in Bournemouth five years ago.'

'They've all been bought in England, then?'

'The handbag is American. Otherwise she must have restocked herself when she returned.'

She frowned, half sensing some illogicality here. 'Had she no personal papers?'

'Your – the murderer destroyed them.'

'But he didn't destroy Nick's two letters.'

'They were hidden in the lining of the violin case.'

Philippa turned and opened the case, lifted out the violin and stared at the torn lining. It was a good violin though rather small, a Grancino, and probably worth a couple of hundred pounds.

'Did she have any money on her? Had she no banking account?'

'None under her own name at any rate.'

Philippa put the violin back and turned over the pieces of music at the bottom of the suitcase. Two or three Mozart and Beethoven sonatas. A series of exercises and the Bach Chaconne. After a moment her fingers stopped and she slipped out a single sheet of manuscript music.

'Was this in with the others?'

'Yes.'

96

It was a simple tune, scored in ink on home-ruled paper. Either Elizabeth had copied it somewhere or she had experimented in composing for herself.

Philippa hummed the tune under her breath. She did not know it.

'Could I have this?' she asked.

'I'm afraid not until after the trial.'

She half put the sheet back, then changed her mind and jotted down the first bars on the back of an envelope. It might be worth trying some music shop.

She felt that Archer was getting impatient, and in fact she knew she had taken up enough of his time. The last thing she wanted to do was to become a nuisance to him so that he would avoid seeing her.

'Thank you,' she said. 'You've been very kind. You'll try to help me about a visit to New York?'

'I'll let you know tomorrow,' he promised.

'This Elena Rusman,' said the Assistant Commissioner, frowning. 'You're quite sure she is not now the same person? That's been confirmed?'

'Yes, sir,' said Archer, flipping through the papers he had brought. 'Final word came just before I phoned you. Elena Rusman left this country in 1942 with the Dutch children of M. van Ruysdael. She stayed in New York with them until last year, when she left them and they lost trace of her. It all seemed to fit in perfectly. But she's now been definitely identified as married and living in Montana. A photograph is being radioed and we should get it tomorrow.'

'It's most confoundly awkward there should have been this slip up,' said the Director of Public Prosecutions. 'It may give the impression that we have been over-precipitate in bringing this man to trial. I don't like that. I shall be seriously inclined to recommend a postponement of the trial for three weeks.'

The Assistant Commissioner said: 'In fact, of course, it doesn't affect the evidence against him in the slightest.'

'Not in the slightest,' agreed the Director. 'But what it might do in the minds of a jury is create a psychological state in which it would seem to them that the police had not been sufficiently thorough. If that occurred we could have all the evidence possible and still fail to send him down.'

The Assistant Commissioner rose and stood warming his hands at the fire. 'I think that's rather taking the gloomy view. What does this discovery amount to? There are about three recent years of Elizabeth Rusman's life unaccounted for, and it is probable she now spent them in England. Well, there's still time before the trial if we don't postpone it. You should be able to do something, Archer. An intensive search will probably produce the necessary results. As I see it, the thing fits together much better now. Quite clearly she found herself with child, perhaps by Talbot, and changed her name and went to live quietly somewhere out of London. That's why her identity card was not renewed in 1943. It's quite possible the child is still alive somewhere, and that she was going to threaten Talbot with a maintenance claim. The case fits together much better without this American red-herring.'

'I'll talk it over with the Attorney-General,' said the Director. 'In the meantime do your best, Archer. If you tie up this loose end you may feel pretty sure of a conviction. If it's left flapping the defence is sure to make a lot of it, for they've precious little to go on at present. That man Tyler is bound to try all his tricks.'

'There's this question of Mrs Talbot wanting to go to

America, sir,' said Archer. 'Clearly we can't let her go on a fool's errand.'

The Assistant Commissioner grunted. 'The facts will come out some time; you'd better give them to the press at once. It's only fair to Talbot, and we've nothing to hide. The more publicity they give it, the easier your work will be.'

'I'll tell Mrs Talbot first thing in the morning,' said Archer.

'See Superintendent Priestley before you go,' the Assistant Commissioner suggested. 'If I were you I should check up on Talbot's army leaves again; I shouldn't be surprised to find that he'd been meeting Elizabeth Rusman more recently than 1942. The new situation may help our case, not Talbot's.'

Chapter Twelve

PHILIPPA'S HEART LEAPT at the news. The knowledge that Elizabeth might have been in England all the time seemed to open up great new possibilities. In an eager meeting with Nick she plagued him vehemently again for all he could tell her about the murdered girl; and though at the end there seemed nothing in all their talk she went away lighter of spirit than she had been for some time. Then after two days more of searching, a chance remark by a woman 'cellist in a ladies' orchestra in Bournemouth sent her hurriedly off eighty miles to a small country town and to a garage owned by a man named Shaw.

There she found to her chagrin that the police had forestalled her only by a matter of a few hours. Mr Shaw, a tough, sandy-complexioned young man with hairy wrists, having been thus officially questioned so recently, was cautious and faintly sly. He couldn't quite believe that Philippa had also come here specially to ask him about the girl he had had an affair with in July, 1942, and kept thrusting back her questions at her as if they were playing some not quite decent party game. Philippa felt hot and humiliated and angry, but persevered until she was sure he had nothing more to tell. He came out with her to the car and held the door open, eyeing her and talking to her about swing music for so long that she was relieved to hear another car hooting behind for petrol.

Though she did not know it until later, the police had quickly got one stage farther than this, having located the doctor and nurse who attended Elizabeth Rusman in

1943. From them they learned that a son had been born to her in April of that year, that the child had died, and no more. In May Elizabeth had left the district, and wartime England had swallowed her up. That she had changed her name was obvious, but the obliging person who had sold her a faked identity and ration card was not forthcoming.

They came to a void, a vacuum, in which no clue or track existed. If Elizabeth Rusman had lived in England during the last three years she had left no trace. It was quite possible, they knew well, that some simple explanation existed to account for no one coming forward, but both the press and themselves were doing all that was possible, and no more could be done.

Once, on the Thursday when they gave *Traviata* for the last time, Philippa sneaked in at the stage-door of Covent Garden and listened from the wings. Ravogli, being cheated of his Philippa, had had the bright idea of engaging another English girl, and Caroline Winthram was singing in her place. She had had good notices, and Philippa listened with terrible feelings of discomfort to the strong sweet voice of her deputy. Her feelings became so intense that she could not stay to the end; and she slipped out as secretly as she had come and called a taxi and went home to the flat. She'd been crazy, she knew now, to go near the place.

She lay on the bed and her mind tried to unthink the happenings of the last weeks, so that instead of being here solitary and bitter she was at Covent Garden on the stage tonight, and Nick in the box again, and all the lovely fruits of long years of struggle were back in her grasp and not rotting in the gutter where she had thrown them.

She lay on the bed with open eyes until the early hours of the morning.

So Thursday became Friday, and Friday ran into the week-end, and the week-end flowered and died and gave way to the dry seed-pod of Monday morning. It was the last week-end before the trial. Worn out, Philippa at last consented to spend it with the Newcombes at their home in Surrey; Nick spent his in Brixton reading *Middlemarch* and smoking interminable cigarettes; Mr Tyler, K.C., golfed with Sir Boyd Dyson, for whom he had once devilled, and Inspector Archer took an hour off to sow another patch of grass. Mr Sidney Fleming read all the Sunday newspapers, in particular the sensational ones, which for once gave him the sort of reading he was looking for.

On the eve of the trial Mr Stephen Tyler had a final conference with Mr Claude Land, who was to be his junior, and Arthur McNeill and Mr Frobisher. When it became known that there was this gap in the murdered woman's history, McNeill, knowing his chief's quick changes of front, would not have been greatly surprised to see him scrap the line of defence they had been working on and use this unexpected flaw in the prosecution's case as part of a new plan.

But Tyler accepted the news with reserve. The police were still working full pressure to fill the gap and might any time succeed. Also it was just as plain to him as to the Director of Public Prosecutions that the weakness was really no weakness in the circumstantial evidence of the crime. It could be made use of, should be made use of, if still available. But there were bolder courses to take.

To attack the reputation and veracity of one of the witnesses for the Crown was a dangerous game. Once done, it enabled the prosecution to attack the reputation of the prisoner, and in ninety-nine cases out of a hundred that would be fatal. Bad faith, debts, previous convictions were the record of most men standing in the box on a capital charge. But Nicolas Talbot's record seemed clean enough, and Tyler's view was that this could be turned to advantage.

'It's all very well,' McNeill said, arguing more on principle than because he was unconvinced. 'But which of us here would like to stand in the box to be cross-examined by Wells on his past life? Nobody's been an angel, certainly not Talbot.'

'D'you think he'll keep his temper?' Land asked.

'Talbot gives me the impression of being a pretty tough character,' said Tyler, rubbing his bald head. 'But likeable. A man who should make a good showing in the box. But in any case it should be worth the risk. Heaven seldom sends one a witness quite like the principal witness for the Crown. With a free hand I'll tear him to shreds.'

'There are – er – certain features of Mr Talbot's life,' said Frobisher in his grey careful voice, 'which might be used against him. Since you indicated to me the line you would take, Mr Tyler, I've questioned Mr Talbot very closely on his past history. He was very frank and full in his account and you have it all set out in the brief. I hope it has not been overlooked.'

'McNeill and I read it through in the early hours of this morning,' said Tyler. 'It can and will be used against him, but I'm convinced it's worth the risk.'

The day of the trial broke warm and sunny. It was the first Thursday in May, and as Philippa looked out of the window of the flat she could hear the sparrows chirping and chattering. It was a day for going out and seeking the first green fields, to walk by a river or to wander in a wood. Middlesex were playing their first match of the season at Lord's.

In the Central Criminal Court at the Old Bailey spring existed on hearsay evidence. Only the brightness of the light falling in through the glass dome suggested that an outer, freer, sunnier air existed somewhere and that all men might not be bent on the grim faded processes of human law.

To Philippa, after a sleepless night of foreboding, the court came as an anticlimax. As at Bow Street, she had expected something bigger and more imposing. This might have been a small county court, drab and yellow and unimpressive and built for the consideration of trespass and petty thefts. Little wonder the policeman said that the long patient queue stretching round the building outside had no hopes of getting in. She was glad of that. The fewer to peer and whisper the better.

Joan and John Newcombe were both there to greet her, and they sat together on one of the front benches. Philippa knew she would have to go into one of the outer rooms as soon as the trial started, since she was an important witness for the defence, but she wanted first to see Nick and to feel the general atmosphere into which she would suddenly be called either late today or early tomorrow.

Presently leading counsel drifted in, and Philippa glanced anxiously at Sir Alfred Wells, K.C., who was leading for the Crown. He was a taller, older, more imposing man than Tyler, with a beak of a nose and a habit of pursing his lips suddenly as if about to say 'shush'. As the benches filled up round her, Philippa's heart began to beat and the old sick feeling returned. She realized that somehow the court was not unimpressive after all. She realized that she was frightened, and getting more frightened, for Nick.

Chapter Thirteen

'YOUR NAME IS Mrs Catherine Evans, and you keep a small private hotel at No. 29A, The Esplanade, Dolgelly?'

'Yes,' said the woman in the box.

'Do you recognize the prisoner?'

'Yes, indeed.'

'Tell us when you met him.'

'Well, he came to stay at my place in the spring of 1942.'

'What name did he use?'

'Talbot he says was his name. And Elizabeth Rusman stayed with him as Mrs Talbot.'

'How did you know she was Elizabeth Rusman?'

'Well, I had seen her playing in a ladies' orchestra at Llandudno the year before and using her maiden name. I told her so to her face and they said they were just married.'

'How long did they stay?'

'Three weeks or nearly so. Then one morning Mr Talbot pays the bill and leaves. The lady stayed on two more days and then she left. Fairly down in the mouth, she was, I assure you.'

Nick yawned. Yes, he was on trial for his life, but the natural reactions would not be balked. The court had grown stuffy as the morning wore on and this early evidence seemed so useless, since it only proved what was already admitted. The first part of the morning, Wells's opening speech had been a different matter. Quietly and without enmity he had given in detail the facts of the Crown's case. Methodically he had woven together the evidence, thread by thread, until it seemed to Nick like a giant net of misapplied testimony that would presently be flung over his head and drawn tight. The old liaison with the murdered woman, the two love letters she had preserved and the locket photograph about her neck, the encounter in the theatre, the assignment to meet, the silver pencil lying on the floor among the debris, the injury to his head and the contradictory stories he had told of how he had received it. . . .

Certain phrases of Wells's speech still rang in Nick's head.

'We cannot say with certainty what Nicolas Talbot's feelings were when Elizabeth Rusman spoke to him behind the stage at Covent Garden. Nor do we need to guess. The evidence, we contend, shows that she was determined at all costs to attempt a renewal of their old intimacy. Not only did she exact the promise of a meeting, but in scribbling her address added a few words which can only be construed as a deliberate threat. "Come," she said in effect, "or I'll make all the trouble I can." Faced with this sudden acute danger to the success of his new marriage, the probability of shipwreck . . .

'This, members of the jury, is the statement made and signed by the prisoner that night in the presence of Inspector Archer and Detective Constable Kellett. May I read you an extract: "I received this injury in a quarrel with my wife. It was a stupid quarrel and no doubt I was very irritating. She threw something at me and I left the house in a temper and walked round the streets for three-quarters of an hour before going into a chemist's shop." But in the early morning, let me remind you, the police went round to Pelham Court to see Mrs Talbot. They found her awake and a little anxious about her husband's absence; but when they questioned her she denied any such quarrel as he had mentioned. Nor was there any evidence of it when later she changed her story to agree with his. . . .'

Wells had gone on: 'What is the next thing the accused man says? "I never at any time that night went near Elizabeth Rusman's flat." Yet on the following morning at Bow Street there was an identification parade of ten men, one being the accused. They were all dressed exactly alike, in trilby hats and raincoats, and all with a bandage over their left temples. Present at this parade was Mike Grieve, the janitor, the only man to see the murderer leave the house. Now among those ten men, whom did he identify? He identified Nicolas Talbot. . . .'

So it had mounted and mounted until there seemed no alternative for the jury but that they should rise at once and pronounce him guilty without wasting more of the court's time.

Now, having said all that, Wells was painstakingly going about the business of proving it. Poor Mrs Evans was dragged away from the Welsh fastnesses of Dolgelly to play her part; stage hands from the Opera House who had witnessed his meeting with Elizabeth, the tall shabby chemist, the young doctor and the young nurse, Inspector Archer and the Divisional Surgeon, Mrs Grieve . . .

At these people Tyler waved a hand or cross-examined briefly. From Archer he established the fact that no finger-prints belonging to the prisoner had been found in the murdered woman's room, and then let him go. On the afternoon resumption Mr Justice Ferguson made everything drag by writing the testimony down in long-hand, and Nick could see the trial running into Tuesday or Wednesday of next week at this rate.

He stole a glance at the jury, and was relieved to find none of them staring at him. On the whole a fairly intelligent group, the exception being a burly red-faced young man in the back row who looked as if he had just come out of prison himself. The three women had been given seats in the front row: two might have been school teachers or civil servants, the other was a motherly soul with a kind eye. The foreman, a man called Pindar, had a nervous sniff that irritated Nick. He wanted to pass a handkerchief along.

Mr Tyler was asking questions. It all seemed very unimportant.

'You say the time you reached your home was about ten minutes past eleven, Mrs Grieve?'

'Yes, sir.'

'Where was your husband when you first saw him?'

'Coming out of the bedroom, gaspin' and chokin' with the smoke.'

'What did he do?'

'He shouts to me: "For Gawd's sake fetch the cops, Maggie, the 'ouse is on fire an' there's been bloody murder done!"'

'Quite,' said Mr Tyler dryly, 'and then I think you ran into the next-door house to telephone?'

'Yes, sir.'

'Was there anyone else about when you first reached your home?'

'No, sir, but by the time I'd done my phoning and got back there was a bob – a policeman there who'd seen the smoke from down the street and come without bein' asked.'

'Thank you, Mrs Grieve.' Tyler sat down.

Her husband was next to be called, and Nick stared with interest at this witness whom he had only seen once before, for a moment at the identification parade. A tough-looking man, worthy companion for that odd juror: coarse red face, a chin built for bristles, eyes screwed up a little as if unused to bright lights.

Sir Alfred Wells was treating him gently, courteously, trying, one suspected, by his deferential attitude to hypnotize the jury into a similar attitude of mind. He went through it all, and Grieve, to do him justice, was a good witness while the expected questions could be met with the well-drilled answers. Nick felt it was all old stuff, but he could see the effect it had on the jury.

Sir Alfred Wells sat down satisfied, and Mr Stephen Tyler got up. He looked at Mr Grieve, blew his nose, and looked at him again reflectively while he stowed the handkerchief away in an under pocket.

'How old are you, Mr Grieve?'

Grieve stared at this new, smaller, wigged figure. He knew all about this one.

'Fifty,' he said in his husky voice.

'Ever been in a witness-box before?'

'No,' said Grieve.

'Have you ever been in a court before?'

There was a moment's hesitation. 'Maybe.'

'The witness-box is not your usual position?'

'Eh?'

'What I mean is that you are more accustomed to standing in the dock?'

'No, I ain't.'

Mr Tyler raised his eyebrows. 'Are you telling the court that you have never been in the dock?'

Grieve looked up at the glass dome.

'Maybe I 'ave.'

'Tell us about your appearance in dock.'

'Which one?'

A murmur of amusement ran round the court.

'Oh, any of them,' said Tyler. 'It doesn't really matter.'

'What's it to do with this case, eh?'

'Precisely,' said Sir Alfred, half rising, 'what I was going to ask Mr Tyler myself. My Lord, I trust Mr Tyler realizes that this constitutes—'

'I fully realize,' said Tyler, 'everything it constitutes, Sir Alfred. Tell us, Mr Grieve, what you were convicted of.'

'Not much, anyway.'

'Shall I refresh your memory. Have you been convicted at least five times of being drunk and disorderly?'

Again Grieve hesitated and glanced at Sir Alfred. But Sir Alfred was not looking.

'Maybe.'

'Answer me yes or no.'

'Yes. . . .'

'Thank you, Mr Grieve. Now will you cast your mind back to your last conviction. Is it true that you were convicted of assaulting a lady?'

This was too much for the witness. 'Well,' he said indignantly, 'I only put me arm round 'er in a bus and the old geyser run me in!'

The murmur was nearer a laugh.

'You were drunk then?'

'No! I was only being friendly!'

There was something in Tyler's manner as he put the next question that quelled the amusement which was moving about the court.

'Were you feeling friendly on the night of the second of April last?'

'What d'yer mean?'

'What time did Elizabeth Rusman come in that night?'

'I've told you. About 'alf ten.'

'How do you know?'

'Because I seen her go in just as I was turning into the pub opposite for a pint.'

'What did you say to her?'

'I didn't say nothing. She never seen me, because it was misty.'

'And what did you do then?'

'Had me pint.'

'Was that before or after you went up to her bedroom?'

'Before, of course.'

'And how many pints did you have?'

'I had two quick ones an' brought two back.'

'Fortifying yourself, I suppose?'

'That's right,' said Grieve, glad he could agree on something.

'At what stage did you start feeling friendly?'

There was a moment's pause while Grieve stared at Tyler. Counsel for the Crown were whispering together. There was no sleepiness in the court now. Tyler's line was quite clear.

'I don't know what you mean,' Grieve said at last.

'At what stage did you start wanting to put your arm round some woman?'

Tyler's line was becoming clear even to Grieve.

'Swelp me, I never did!' he exclaimed indignantly.

'Well, tell us this. When you came back from fortifying yourself at the public house, how many women were there in the house?'

'Which 'ouse?'

'Yours.'

'Why, only . . . 'er.'

'Only Elizabeth Rusman. She was a pretty young woman, wasn't she?'

Grieve's eye roamed uneasily about.

'Yes, she was all right.'

'Nice enough for you?'

'Look,' said Mike Grieve in a hoarse whisper. 'What yer—'

But his answer was partly lost because Sir Alfred was on his feet again addressing the judge. It was, he said, his duty to protest most vigorously against Mr Tyler's line of cross-examination. It seemed, said Sir Alfred, that Mr Tyler was not now satisfied with attacking the credibility of the witness but was implying, etc., etc. Hypocritically Mr Tyler stood his ground and said he was implying nothing. It was very far from his business to accuse this witness or any witness of the murder of Elizabeth Rusman. His duty was to his client and his client only. And his client, he would remind Sir Alfred, stood in the dock fighting for life and liberty. In such circumstances, said Mr Tyler, he would be grossly and personally negligent of his duty if he did not probe this astonishing weakness in the Crown's case to its very depths, etc., etc. Then the judge discussed the matter with them at some length, and in the end the issue seemed somehow to become not who had killed Elizabeth Rusman but what Lord Justice Bretherton had said in the Court of Criminal Appeal in 1921. Presently Mr Tyler conceded some point and Sir Alfred sat down and the judge picked up his pen and Mr Tyler turned his attention to Mike Grieve with undiminished venom.

'Did you like Miss Rusman?'

'. . . She was all right. What I seen of her.'

'You didn't see as much of her as you would have liked?'

'I tell you, she wasn't my sort!'

'Wasn't worth the risk, I suppose?'

'Eh?'

'Not when sober.'

'Oh, I was sober enough.'

'So you went out to get a little courage.'

'I went out to get a pint!'

'You mean four pints.'

'Well, yes . . .'

The man was sweating now.

'And when you came back, duly fortified and feeling friendly, how long was it before you started thinking of the lonely woman upstairs?'

'I didn't! I shouldn't have thought nothing about her if I 'adn't seen the man coming out as I was going in!'

'What man?'

Grieve lifted up a short fat forefinger and pointed at Nick. 'That man!'

'How did you recognize him?' Tyler asked quietly.

'When?'

'When you met him.'

'I didn't. I never seen him before.'

'Are you sure you saw him then?'

'What?'

'Are you sure there was any man there at all?'

'Course I am! Think I was dreaming?'

'No, I think you'd had four pints and were feeling friendly. I put it to you that you were far more interested in Elizabeth Rusman than in any man you may or may not have passed on the stairs.'

Grieve stared into the prominent handsome eyes of the counsel. 'I weren't! I tell you I weren't! I only went up to see what was amiss.'

'How did you know there was anything amiss?'

'I didn't, but I smelt a rat.'

'You mean to say you went upstairs to see if anything was wrong merely because you saw a man coming down?'

'Well, 'e'd got blood on 'is 'andkerchief.'

'How did you know which door to go to?'

'I'd seen Rusman come in. I knew there was no one else in the 'ouse.'

So it went on. Without pause but without haste Tyler went on to Grieve's discovery of the body, calling in question step by step each part of his testimony. If it had not been for the fact that this man had, apparently with wilful malice, wrongly identified him, Nick would have felt sorry for Grieve. Tyler came to the arrival of Mrs Grieve on the scene, and by the phrasing of his questions suggested to the jury that, far from trying to put the fire out, Mike Grieve might well have been surprised in the act of burning down the house.

At last Tyler stopped for a few moments to collect his notes and Grieve, wiping his sweating face with a red handkerchief, made a half move to go. But Tyler stopped him.

'Not yet, Mr Grieve. I haven't quite finished. You have given us your version of what happened before the police arrived. What happened when the police were in charge? Did they examine the body and the room and take a statement from you?'

'That's right.'

'Where were you when you gave them this statement?'

'Sittin' on a chair.'

'In the room where the murder was committed?'

'That's right.'

'Did you see what went on in the room?'

'They was asting me questions all the time.'

'Did you see the doctor take a locket from round the dead woman's neck?'

'I seen 'im give it to the police.'

'Was it open?'

'The inspector opened it.'

'Did he show it to the doctor?'

'That's right.'

'Did you see the photograph inside?'

'What, me? No.'

'Could you have seen it if you'd wanted to?'

'I dunno.'

'You don't remember?'

'That's right.'

Tyler hesitated a second. There were other questions he could put, but his sense of timing told him that this was the moment to sit down. He was conscious of the impression all this had made. He sat down and listened to the excited whispers of his colleague.

Mike Grieve, thankful at almost any price to escape from the witness-box, was turning to go when he was again recalled.

'Just one word more, Mr Grieve,' said Sir Alfred Wells. 'I understand that one pint of your beer was untouched when you discovered the fire. That means you had only drunk three. Now can you tell us approximately how many pints you had taken the day you put your arm round the lady in the bus?'

Grieve gazed at him sheepishly. 'Oh ... I dunno. About eight or ten. ...'

Wells breathed again. He had been hoping that his witness would see the point of the question.

'So I imagine it takes considerably more than three pints to put you over the mark?'

'Not 'arf, it don't!'

The judge lowered his pen and looked at Grieve distastefully. 'Not half, it don't. Will you kindly tell the court whether that means yes or no.'

'My Lord,' said Wells, 'I think the witness means that it takes very much more than three pints.'

'That's right, m'Lord. That's what I said.'

'Now between the night that you found the body and the morning when you identified the prisoner, how much liquor did you drink?'

'Not a drop,' said Grieve fervently.

'Did you *at any time* see the photograph in the locket?'

'No!'

'Did you *at any time* speak to Elizabeth Rusman on the night of the murder?'

'No!'

'Thank you, Mr Grieve.' While the man was at last escaping, Wells was thoughtfully fingering his shabby gown. 'My Lord,' he said, 'in view of the suggestions put forward by Mr Tyler in the course of his cross-examination, I ask your permission to recall Inspector Archer to the witness-stand.'

Tyler and Land had their heads together. Both of them had foreseen this move. But the judge glanced at the clock.

'You may recall him tomorrow, Sir Alfred,' he said, and rose.

The first day was over.

Chapter Fourteen

FOUR HUNDRED AND NINE miles away Mr Sidney
Fleming was reading the London papers which had just
come in.

From where he was sitting he should have been able to
hear C Form at their chanting under Mr Duncan – if the
boys of C Form had not been scattered to the four
corners of the kingdom and Mr Duncan, with sour
patient enterprise, on a walking tour in Snowdonia.

The school clock chimed two-thirty and Fleming
folded the papers on his desk. He put on his gown and
went out. All the classrooms were empty and he met
nobody, strolling through the various rooms of the
school.

During this Easter vacation he had taken very much to
spending his time in the school proper and neglecting his
own house. Another might have found something eerie
and uncomfortable about the big deserted building with
the chapel and the new gymnasium attached. Seething and
murmuring with life during term-time, it was now
echoing and draughty and cold. Dawns came up and
nights fell upon the dusty class-rooms, and nothing
stirred within them except the one silent lonely man
pacing through them thinking his lonely thoughts.

But for him his own house was the one to be shunned.
Matron had as usual gone off at the end of the term, and a
day later he had told Mrs Turnbull not to come again
until the school reassembled, as he was going away himself. At that time he had toyed with the idea of visiting his
cousin in Birmingham; but it had come to nothing. So

except for McLeod, the lodge-keeper, he was quite alone at the school. Not that he minded that, for he loved the school with all his heart.

The trouble with his own house was that he had not been able to move anything. Her bed was beside his own, the lamp-shade she had made still on the bedside light. He had cleared away the magazines – the empty, saccharine magazines with their society photos and their theatre talk; they'd always been a bone of contention – but the powder bowl, the pin-cushion, the half-empty jar of face cream he had not liked to move. A pair of shoes were still under the bed and a dressing-gown hung behind the door. And there was the wardrobe full of her clothes – clothes she had bought with his money and had left behind, it seemed, as a last contemptuous gesture. Even now that Mrs Turnbull did not come he had left them alone. The silent inanimate symbols of her being were uncomfortable to him, but he was strong enough to prefer them to the risk of comment. For two weeks he had endured her photograph on the piano downstairs; but one day when Mrs Turnbull was in the room he had contrived to brush it off with his sleeve so that the glass broke.

Soon, one more term, he would be leaving it all. Not too soon. It couldn't be a moment too soon.

Today he had read the papers with eager interest for any information about the opening of the trial. They really said very little, and, being so far away, he must wait until tomorrow to get any news of its progress.

A weaker man, he knew, might have gone to London, for there was nothing to tie him here until the school reassembled next week. He might even have queued to watch the trial. But such a move would have been against his principles, and principle with him was always the strongest moving force. Never in all his life had he pushed, queued, forced himself, been moved by mob sentiment, curiosity, panic, to do the illogical, silly or conventional thing. Even in the crisis a month ago this inner calm had stood by him. Always he had acted as his reason told him. (Well, always except that once, and then she had provoked him as so often before, and this time beyond the limits.)

He went into the chapel and shut the heavy door behind him and sat down on one of the pitch-pine pews. (Always there was a little skimping of the refinements, a cheese-paring tendency in Lady Clunes's generosity; a crying pity that this grand chapel had not been given the bench ends it deserved.)

He had spent many hours in here this last fortnight, impervious to the chill striking up from the stone floor. Between himself and God there were no secrets, and he had soberly faced the issues in his soul. Sometimes he was touched with feelings of horror and remorse, but that was when he woke up in the night, when the soft, emotional, conscience-ruled springs of his mind were freed from the censors of reason and logic. Here in the chapel with God to help him and his mind clear there was no such weakness: he had come to see that his killing of her was the only thing that could have happened; of two bitter evils he had chosen the lesser, not only on selfish grounds but on grounds of spiritual fitness. If one of two people had to go, then the one who was morally useless to the community must go before the one who was useful. That was surely as true on Christian as on Nietzschean principles.

Even Talbot's unexpected arrest was not impossible to fit into the pattern, though had it been anyone else he would have been faced with a very different problem.

Today he could not settle in his usual manner to an hour

or so in the quiet. It was the Thing going on in London and the knowledge that any time now six copies of the *Edinburgh Evening News* would be delivered at Angus Baird's, the general shop in the village. One was for the rector, one for Dr Wishart, three others for regular customers. One sometimes was unsold or was read by Baird himself. Fleming never bought one. It was a principle of his to disapprove of the silly habit which needed the world's news twice a day.

He was wondering now whether his calling in for a paper at Baird's would be so unusual as to invite remark. He was wondering whether a Scottish evening paper would carry any early information of the progress of the trial.

He decided that it might. He decided that the risk was very small.

He rose and left the chapel.

Chapter Fifteen

FRIDAY WAS MORE cloudy, and in the court-room the alternating sun and shadow was like the passing of a great hand ever and again across the glass dome.

The newspapers had made a lot of Mr Tyler's unexpected move, and if he had been craving publicity for his future in law he could have chosen no better way. But in justice to Mr Tyler, his only aim was the acquittal of his client.

The morning saw a duel between Archer and Tyler. Archer was of different stuff from Grieve, and if anything the case for the defence lost ground as a result of the Inspector's recall. Archer was unshakable in his statement that under no circumstances could Grieve have seen the photograph in the locket, and somehow made his case the stronger by freely admitting that there had been some irregularity on the part of the police in allowing Grieve to remain in the room during the first minutes of their inquiries. Knowing that his attack on Grieve would almost certainly mean Archer's recall, Tyler had saved his cross-examination until now, and the morning was far gone before Archer stood down and the prosecution's case was closed.

Then it was Mr Tyler's turn again. He began in his conversational easy manner.

'You have been told, members of the jury, that the defence will assail the Crown's evidence for being all of a circumstantial nature. Well, you have been told wrong. My complaint, as I am sure yours must be too, is that the evidence is not circumstantial enough. At first sight it may look quite a formidable case; but on closer examination how plainly one sees everywhere the element of doubt! The defence, of course, is a complete denial of the story.

'You shall hear what really happened to the accused that night. A simple ordinary quarrel between himself and his wife, such as any of us might have. That is all. Nothing more. And only one person's evidence, mark you, to contradict Nicolas Talbot's story. You are asked to believe Grieve's word before that of the prisoner: that is the issue and nothing more than that.

'I have already been asked whether I am attempting to level any direct accusation against this man Grieve. Let me say, as I have said before, that it is no part of my duty to provide the police with alternative hypotheses for this murder. It is not for me to prove the guilt of another man – though I propose with the court's permission to call one witness whose evidence you may think has a significant bearing on this point. It may even occur to you that, whatever the truth, Grieve with his history would naturally be personally concerned in seeing the suspicion diverted to someone else. That is not for me to say. But let me remind you of another thing. It is not even for me to prove the innocence of the man you see in the dock. The whole onus of proof lies upon the Crown, who must prove Talbot's guilt *beyond all doubt* before you can bring in a verdict against him.'

Nick listened with a growing sense of comfort. One's spirits, one's hopes, constantly wavered between two extremes as the witnesses and the speakers came and went. When Tyler was on his feet he felt as good as a free man. When Wells rose he could smell Brixton again and feel the tightening of the rope.

He looked at the first witness for the defence in some surprise. So did most of the others in court. The tradition is well established that on a capital charge the defending counsel shall call the prisoner first. But Mr Tyler was not afraid of tradition.

As for Nick he had never seen this witness before.

'Your name is Jonah Hartley and you live at No. 46, Loften Street?'

'Yes.'

'You rent the room immediately above the one in which the murder took place?'

'Yes.'

'Tell us what happened on the afternoon of the 28th March.'

'Well, I was just going off to work – I work nights, see, and I was coming down the stairs when I heard raised voices in Miss Rusman's room and the door was half open, and as I passed I heard Miss Rusman say: "I'm not interested in what you think or feel, Mr Grieve. Kindly get out of this bedroom or I'll call the police." '

So this was the one witness, thought Nick.

'Go on, Mr Hartley.'

'Well, it not being my business, like, I was for going on, being a peaceable man; but just then Miss Rusman must have heard me passing, for she came to the door and called me in.'

'What did you find?'

'Grieve was standing by the mantelpiece looking red and awkward, and Miss Rusman was really angry, I could see that. She says to me, "Mr Hartley, would you please see Mr Grieve downstairs. He was just leaving," she says. So I waits a moment and then Grieve comes along and slouches off out without saying a word to either of us. Then Miss Rusman thanked me and I went too.'

'Thank you, Mr Hartley.'

Sir Alfred was at once on his feet.

'Was there anything in what you saw to suggest that Grieve had been pressing his attentions on Miss Rusman?'

'Well . . . she was certainly angry about something.'

'From what you saw or heard, might they not have been having words over another matter, say that Mr Grieve had gone up to ask for some back rent and Miss Rusman had refused to pay it?'

'Well . . . it didn't look like that to me.'

'I am not asking you what it looked like. I am asking you for a plain answer, yes or no. Was there anything you heard or saw inconsistent with a quarrel over the rent or some other ordinary matter?'

Hartley hesitated. 'Maybe not.'

'Can you say that it could not have been such a quarrel?'

'. . . No.'

Sir Alfred sat down. Mr Tyler got up.

'Mr Hartley, if you were behind in your rent and the landlord came up to ask for back money, would you threaten him with the police?'

'No.'

'No,' said Mr Tyler, 'I thought not,' and sat down.

A succession of minor witnesses followed. First an analyst who told of the discovery of glass particles in a rug in Talbot's bedroom. Then a series of people came forward to testify to the prisoner's good character. This Nick found the most embarrassing part of the trial, but Tyler had insisted on taking full advantage of his gamble. This saw the luncheon break through and it was not until the middle of the afternoon that there was a brief pause and a voice said:

'Mrs Talbot . . .'

'Mrs Talbot . . .'

Nick felt his mouth go dry.

She came in steadily enough and took her place in the

witness-box, repeating the oath in a low clear voice. On the lapel of the severely tailored black suit she was wearing was the diamond clip he had given her for Christmas. In her pocket, though he did not know it, was the crystal elephant he had given her six weeks ago.

Once, just for a moment, she glanced at Nick and their eyes met. Then she turned to her counsel.

Mr Tyler was very kind. Seeing her so nervous to begin, he led off with a number of soothing and largely irrelevant questions to give her time to get her bearings. Everybody in the court seemed to be sitting forward to hear Philippa's evidence.

Gently the story came round to the night of the opera, the meeting with Elizabeth Rusman, the quarrel.

'In short, Mrs Talbot, remembering that you are on oath, you can state quite definitely that you alone were responsible for your husband's head injury on the night of the murder?'

'I swear it.'

'Thank you.' Tyler abruptly sat down. The evening before he had said to Land, 'Let Wells do the questioning. He won't find it easy.'

But Wells realized just as well as Tyler how easy it would be to lose the sympathy of the jury if he tried to harass this witness.

With the utmost courtesy he began:

'This quarrel you say you had with your husband. What was it about?'

'It wasn't really about anything. I was in a tired nervous state ready to be upset by almost anything. I really can hardly remember what began it.'

'Yet it went so far, you say, that you threw a large glass bottle at him and cut his head open?'

Philippa glanced down at the box.

'Yes . . . I'm ashamed to say.'

'If I may say so, Mrs Talbot, you look a reasonable woman. But that is surely an unreasonable act you are confessing to?'

Philippa said: 'I – I lost my temper. You see, my husband – '

'One thing at a time, please. Would you or would you not describe it as an unreasonable act?'

'I certainly think it was, now.'

'You won't blame us, therefore, if we look on it in that light?'

'No,' she said, and then quickly: 'But I did do it.'

'Did this – er – quarrel arise from seeing your husband's meeting with Elizabeth Rusman that evening?'

'That more or less began it, yes.'

'Did you resent the meeting?'

'A little.'

'And you say that your husband, after receiving the injury, at once put on his hat and coat and went out?'

'Yes.'

'Not even stopping to examine or tie up the injury?'

'He was naturally angry and went straight out.'

'Was it bleeding much?'

'A little.'

'But when the police came there was no blood to show?'

'No, he left so quickly that there was no blood in the flat. He took his handkerchief with him.'

'Nor was there a single sign of this quarrel in the way of stains or broken glass or corroborative evidence from a neighbour – that is – er – apart from the microscopic dust a witness has been at pains to discover?'

'I cleaned it up,' said Philippa. 'I've told you what happened.'

Mr Justice Ferguson leaned forward.

'You ask us to believe that this bitter quarrel took place and left no evidence of any sort you could show the police?'

She turned, gripping the box 'My Lord, I washed out my things which were stained with the lotion and mopped it up off the floor, which is of oak. I brushed the broken glass into a piece of newspaper and carried it downstairs to the incinerator.'

'Why were you so anxious to remove all traces of the affair?' asked his Lordship.

'I was very sorry – and ashamed of what I'd done. I was expecting my husband back and I purposely tried to leave no sign of any quarrel. Home-comings are important, aren't they, my Lord?'

For a few seconds a pair of faded but alert brown eyes stared into a pair of very clear hazel ones. The judge was the first to look away.

'Go on, Sir Alfred.'

'In the first place, Mrs Talbot, you denied ever having had this quarrel with your husband. Why?'

'That was only because I wanted to keep it to myself – just as he did.'

Wells puffed out his lips, as if about to say 'shush' to the whole court. 'Mrs Talbot,' he said gently, 'I am going to put a suggestion to you. You need not answer it if you don't wish to. We all appreciate your grief at your husband's plight; you are no doubt still in love with him and are greatly concerned for the outcome of the trial. I am going to suggest to you that you did quarrel with your husband that evening, that he forced the quarrel on you in order to have a pretext for leaving you and going out. But I suggest that there is no truth in the story of your having thrown something at him, that he put forward this falsehood to explain the injury, and that you are supporting him out of a mistaken sense of loyalty.'

Philippa said 'That isn't so! It did happen just as I've said. My Lord, I've told only the truth.'

Damn this trial! Nick thought. Damn that great fat crow with his tattered black gown. Standing there well fed and shabby and self-righteous.

Someone touched his shoulder and he shook off the hand. Why couldn't the man—?

'Nicolas Talbot!' said a loud voice, and a hand grasped his arm so that this time it could not be dislodged.

Nick looked across and saw that the witness-stand was empty. He looked at the warder beside him. It was his turn at last.

Chapter Sixteen

HE FOUND HIMSELF facing rows of hungry faces to whom previously he had only shown his back. He stared at them woodenly. Philippa was in court now, that was one comfort. She was sitting between John and Joan Newcombe. He could see them all and was conscious of their feelings without directly looking at them. Mike Grieve was there too.

I wonder, he thought, if Grieve really did it. I wonder if Tyler's move was good detection as well as good law. . . . Somehow it would have been easier to believe if Grieve had looked more of a villain and less of a fool. A perfect specimen of the small-time tough. But would he ever have had the guts to kill a woman with his hands? Knowing Elizabeth, Nick would have thought her able to handle this man without anyone's help. Grieve surely would not have come off unscratched, as apparently he had done.

No, for all Tyler's cleverness, he was inclined to believe Grieve's story of the man coming down the stairs. And he was afraid the jury would do the same. Fortunately an accused man, through his counsel, could claim the best of both worlds. It was perfectly fair defence to imply in one breath that Grieve did it, and add in the next, 'But if you don't believe that, then you must believe in an unknown man X whom Elizabeth Rusman knew during the three missing years.'

And Philippa thought, so far they say the case has gone fairly well, and I can see by their eyes that they aren't deceiving me. If we come through this and he's free I swear I'll shoot myself before I ever quarrel with him again. Keep your fingers crossed, Nick. God, don't let that fat man twist it all back again.

It was nearly That Fat Man's turn. Tyler had four more questions to ask.

'What was your reason for telling those different stories to the chemist and the doctor?'

'In each case I made the first excuse that came into my head. I'd no wish to go into details of a family quarrel.'

'This message Elizabeth Rusman scribbled on your programme. Did you know of its existence?'

'I knew she had written her address down for me. I put it straight into my pocket and never looked at it.'

'If you had read the message, would you have construed it as a threat?'

'Of course not. Elizabeth wasn't in the least the sort of person to threaten anyone.'

'Finally, did you see or speak to Elizabeth Rusman again after leaving her at the theatre?'

'I never saw her again.'

'Thank you, Mr Talbot.'

There was a stir in court. The usher looked at the clock. There was still a little time to go.

Nick stared at Wells, who was standing there pushing out his lips at him.

'Mr Talbot, did you love Elizabeth Rusman?'

Nick's eyes did not waver. It was a nasty question at the outset.

'How do you mean?'

'I should have thought the question a simple one.'

Simple but double-edged. 'At one time I was – fond of her. I never loved her as I love my wife.'

'You loved for a little and then tired. So you slipped

130

away and left her, and that was all – so far as you were concerned?'

'If you wish to put it that way.'

'Don't the facts put it that way?'

Quietly now. This was a different Wells from the one who had cross-examined Philippa. Terribly polite still, but with a little hidden sneer behind his eyes.

'Yes, I suppose so,' Nick said.

'Don't you usually find that in such circumstances the lady is inclined to make trouble?'

'What do you imply?'

'Well, surely this is not the only case of its kind you've had experience of?'

'Of that kind, yes.'

'Come, Mr Talbot. The only one?'

'I suppose you could say there was one other.'

'You suppose you could say there was one other.' Sir Alfred took a slip of paper out of his brief.

'Might I crave your Lordship's permission to read a number of names from this paper?'

Mr Justice Ferguson inclined his head.

Sir Alfred read out five names.

'Do these names mean anything to you, Mr Talbot?'

'Some of them.'

'Not all of them?'

'Not all of them in the sense you mean. I knew two of them well, three of them less well.'

'Your memory is bad, Mr Talbot?'

'Not in the least,' Nick said icily. 'But is there any point in bringing up the name of every girl I've taken out to dinner?'

He caught a glint in Sir Alfred's eye. So counsel was not above being irritated by the contemptuous answer.

'Not "taken out to dinner", no. I agree that would be

131

an impossible task. But are you saying you knew these five women no better than that?'

'I knew them better than that. . . . But they . . .'

'Go on.'

'Were the ordinary sort of flirtation. . . . Not at all important. . . .'

'In other words, your affair with the murdered woman was of some importance in your life?'

'Certainly more than those.'

'You will agree that it was important to her.'

'My Lord,' said Tyler, half rising, 'how can the witness judge what Elizabeth Rusman felt in the matter?'

'My Lord,' said Wells, 'I think the existence of the letters and the locket give us direct evidence of the importance she attached to her love affair with Nicolas Talbot.'

Mr Justice Ferguson looked over his glasses. 'Do we then need the witness's concurrence?'

'I submit, my Lord, that the prisoner knew all along that Elizabeth Rusman loved him deeply; and my submission is that the callousness of his earlier conduct towards her was all of a piece with his behaviour on the night of the murder.'

'Very well, Sir Alfred. Go on.'

Wells turned his beak round to the witness-box.

'Did your wife know of your early liaison with Elizabeth Rusman?'

'No, of course not.'

'Of course not? Why didn't you tell her?'

'It was long past, and it didn't occur to me to do so.'

'Do you think she would have married you if she had known?'

'I'm certain of it.'

'Yet on the evening of her learning of it, according to

your story, you had a most violent quarrel and she threw something at your head?'

'Yes.'

'Tell me, Mr Talbot, did you ever promise to marry Elizabeth Rusman?'

'No.'

'At least she didn't have it in black and white, eh?'

'She didn't have it that way or any other way.'

'But those two letters she kept. Perhaps it might at this point be worth glancing again at what the letters have to say.' He paused a moment while the letters were handed to him. Then he caused them to be passed on to Nick. 'Perhaps you would kindly read us the one dated five years ago last month; the marked passage, please.'

Nick stared at the letter. The court waited expectantly. His eyes for a second moved to Philippa, and he saw her looking at him with an expression that seemed to say, "D'you think *I* care what you said to her five years ago. Go on, Nick; it won't hurt me."

' "My very sweet Elizabeth," ' he began in a low voice. ' "Life here without you is proving even more impossible than I thought. Your letters are a help, but precious little compensation for the long days without you. I begin to believe you were right in saying we should never part at all. At this particular moment I feel very sure you are. . ." '

'Thank you, Mr Talbot. Don't those words constitute an offer of marriage?'

'They might have suggested it.'

'Can you tell the court that you never at any time contemplated marriage with Elizabeth Rusman?'

'No, I can't say that.'

'Now let us turn to the writing on the programme. You say in your evidence you never saw the message Elizabeth Rusman wrote under her address, and that even if you had seen it you wouldn't have thought of it as a threat?'

'Certainly not. How could it have been?'

'Does the message convey nothing to you at all?'

'Yes, she was obviously urging me to go to see her.'

'And "Alas! the love of women!"?'

Nick said: 'Oh, yes. It's from Byron.'

'Tell us what that conveys to you.'

'When we were – away together we . . .' He hesitated: '. . . we read Don Juan.' Why did these admissions sound so humiliatingly silly in a court of law. ' "Alas the love of women!" became rather a joke between us. Elizabeth used often to quote it.'

'And what do you think might have been her purpose in putting it on the programme?'

'She must have wanted to remind me of the time we'd spent together.'

'As you know your Byron, Mr Talbot, perhaps you can complete the stanza for me.'

'I've no idea how it goes on.'

'Sure?'

Nick stared at the other man.

'I've told you. I've no idea how it goes on.'

'Perhaps she expected you to remember.'

'Does it matter?'

'It does most emphatically. Let me refresh your memory.' Sir Alfred pouted his lips at his junior who hastily handed him a leather volume open at the right place. Sir Alfred began to read:

> '*Alas! the love of women*' *it is known*
> *To be a lovely and a fearful thing;*
> *For all of theirs upon that die is thrown,*
> *And if 'tis lost, life hath no more to bring*
> *To them but mockeries of the past alone.*'

Here he paused, and added the last lines with some deliberation:

> '*And their revenge is as the tiger's spring,*
> *Deadly and quick and crushing. . . .*'

Wells glanced at the jury to see if they had taken in its significance, then turned again to Nick.

'I put it to you that there was a very definite threat implied in the writing on the programme. I put it to you that you were terrified that Elizabeth Rusman intended to cause a break between you and your wife.'

'I wasn't in the least terrified,' Nick said. 'The idea's quite absurd.'

When Wells spoke again it seemed to be on a new tack. 'Will you tell the court the nature of your present employment.'

Nick had been half expecting this. 'At present I am acting as agent for my wife in arranging concert tours and generally represent her in a business capacity.'

'I see. Then all the money she earns comes into your hands?'

'It goes *through* my hands. I take a small percentage and the rest goes straight into her personal account.'

'Apart from this income from your wife, what other personal money have you?'

Nick hesitated and glanced at the judge. 'Is that necessary, my Lord?'

Mr Justice Ferguson's pen came to a stop. 'I think it's a relevant question.'

'I have about two thousand pounds in cash and certain shares in an East African mining syndicate.'

Sir Alfred considered the answer. 'Not a big fortune as fortunes go.'

'Not as yours goes, perhaps.'

Careful! Nick, thought Philippa. Careful, darling.

Sir Alfred had turned to the judge.

'My Lord, I ask to be protected from such unwarranted remarks.'

His Lordship said severely: 'You must answer the questions in a proper manner, Mr Talbot.'

'Yes, my Lord,' said Nick, 'if they are put in a proper manner.'

The judge continued to look at him.

'I don't think this attitude will help you.'

Nick, Nick, thought Philippa, have patience.

'Your father, I understand, was Brigadier Talbot, a soldier of some repute. Is it true that you were on bad terms with him?'

'Far from it. On the whole we got on well together.'

'On the whole. But you had strong differences of opinion?'

'Yes. Chiefly over a matter of my career.'

'Why was that?'

'He wanted me to become a professional soldier like himself. I wanted to become an engineer.'

'But you are not an engineer?'

'No. Unhappily, we compromised by my becoming neither.'

'How much money did your father leave you?'

'About ten thousand pounds.'

'Most of which you spent?'

'Most of which I spent,' Nick said contemptuously. He wasn't going to go into details of the mining company that had failed.

'Tell me, Mr Talbot, have you ever worked regularly in your life?'

Mr Tyler got up. 'My Lord, I hope Sir Alfred has not forgotten that Mr Talbot has just been demobilized after a distinguished war service of five years – and that he is now only thirty. It doesn't leave a great deal of time for him to have worked regularly – or even irregularly – at anything else.'

Sir Alfred amended his question. 'Would it be true to say, Mr Talbot, that in the few years prior to the war you were a bit of a rolling stone?'

'I travelled a certain amount.'

'And gathered no moss?'

'I made no money.'

'Far from making money, you spent your father's.'

'I invested it unfortunately.'

'So that when you met Miss Shelley you had only a couple of thousand to your name?'

'Yes.'

'Just enough to make a show on?'

'I didn't marry my wife for her money, if that's what you mean.'

Joan Newcombe put her hand on her sister-in-law's arm.

Nick added: 'When I married my wife she had less money than I had.'

'But a big future?'

'It was not at all assured.'

'It was assured on the night Elizabeth Rusman appeared suddenly at Covent Garden?'

'I'm glad to say it was.'

'So that, in the event of a break up of your marriage, you then stood to lose not merely your wife's affections but her money as well?'

'There was no possibility whatever of a break up of our marriage.'

'*If* there was a break up,' said Wells, 'did you or did you not stand to lose financially?'

'I stood to lose far more than that.'

'But you did stand to lose financially.'

Nick said angrily: 'Yes!'

Wells, satisfied, glanced again at his brief, but Mr Justice Ferguson had laid down his pen.

'I think, Sir Alfred, that would be a suitable place at which to adjourn.'

He stood up.

The second day was over.

Chapter Seventeen

BEFORE HE WAS taken back to Brixton for the week-end Philippa managed to get ten minutes with Nick. It was a matter largely at the discretion of the authorities, and in this case the authorities said yes. Philippa suspected Archer had had something to do with it.

She smiled at Nick with lips that were trying to look confident, and then he held her close. They forgot the attendant warder and knew only that they were together again. He was not lost yet – they both knew he was not lost – but they both felt it was going to be touch and go. As she came out of court she had heard a strange barrister say, 'So Tyler's gamble isn't going to come off after all.' And another one replied, 'Still it was quite the best use of the poor material.'

Nick mustn't know that.

'That beastly counsel and his cheap sneers!' she said.

'Cheap but effective.'

'Oh, I don't think so. I don't really, my darling.'

Nick said: 'Wells knows his juries. He's rubbed it in about my immorality for all he's worth, and he's also got it firmly planted in their minds that I intended to live exclusively off you. There'll be all the week-end for it to sink in, then on Monday he'll really get going. D'you realize he's not even *come* to the crime yet.'

'You're looking on the black side. It isn't so. You mustn't doubt for a single moment. There's only one possible result to this trial, and we know it.'

'I wish the jury knew it.'

'They do. Really they do. And on Monday or Tuesday they'll say so.'

He said: 'Those first weeks in Naples, it didn't occur to me that I couldn't meet you clear-mindedly, that I was still likely to be dragging along the trivial tag ends of things finished and done with years before. I should have realized it, but I'm ashamed to say I didn't.'

She smiled back at him. 'Oh, nonsense. . . .'

'No . . . Not nonsense, Philippa. But it's really a question of having a few adventures when one's young, and being unsophisticated enough at the time to think them gay and romantic. It isn't really until one of them comes home to roost in a court of law that it's made to look tawdry and vulgar.'

'Everything looks tawdry in a court of law.'

'No,' said Nick. 'Not everything.'

There was a moment's silence. Time was passing.

'Joan sends her love,' she said quickly. 'I'm spending the week-end down there again. Next week we'll go down together. From then on we'll really start everything over afresh.'

'Phil, I want to say . . . that one thing's stood the strain of these weeks, hasn't it.'

'Nick, did you ever have the least doubt?'

'Not doubt,' he said. 'I knew it. But I didn't know it all. From the first moment you've been a rock. You've never doubted for an instant, have you?'

Philippa did not answer.

'Well, there's something I want you to promise me. Whichever way this turns out, you must look on it as an interlude in your life. Whichever way *I* come out of it, you're too important to get twisted so young. I want to be by you always, giving you love and support. But if by any chance I'm not . . .'

'You must be. Promise you will be.'

'I will be,' said Nick. 'Some way.'

'Good-bye, my love.'

'Good-bye.'

Philippa went out.

She went out of the prisoners' room and out of the Old Bailey to John and Joan Newcombe who were waiting for her; and fifty minutes' run in a car took them to their home in Surrey, where the trees were just in their first green and a cow lowed at milking-time. And the two scenes just did not belong to the same planet: they existed jointly in Philippa's mind and had contact nowhere else.

She slept fitfully and woke at last just after dawn, to find rain dripping on the window. She dressed listlessly, watching the downpour, and spent the morning helping Joan to put up a rufflette rail over the window of Leslie's bedroom.

Somehow the presence of Leslie whistling and chattering about the house was a comfort. Here was the normal, the ordinary, the unimpressed. Leslie knew all about Uncle Nick, but he was at an age when the life in him could not be contained. Cork him down at one point and he bubbled out at another.

It rained the whole day. Joan said it was the only drawback to living in the country; you couldn't get away from the weather. A tonic when the sun shone, a liability when everything dripped and splashed and wept.

In the afternoon they sat over tea a long time. Cheated of his golf, John was working on *The Times* crossword. Leslie was busy with his stamp album, carrying on a muttered conversation with himself, since none of his elders was willing to be drawn in. Joan and Philippa had talked over the trial for the *n*th time. Joan believed now that Mike Grieve had committed the crime, but Philippa, like Nick, was doubtful. It was the sort of thing that could have happened, but some instinct told her it hadn't.

At last Joan said: 'We're getting no further! I confess I'm desperately anxious. Let's try and forget it for the time being. Won't you sing something?'

Philippa said: 'I couldn't. I think I've lost my voice altogether.'

Nevertheless, once suggested, the lure of the piano was not to be put aside; and a bit later she went across to it. She couldn't sing; but instead she played part of Schubert's G Major Sonata.

Even her fingers were stiff, as if they had not touched a piano for years. Drearily, uneasily she browsed through a few of her earlier pieces and then fell silent.

Leslie said: 'Where's Venny-zu-eela, Dad?'

John looked up: 'Um? Venezuela. In South America. You'll get jam on your stamps that way.'

'Daddy, look at this head. The postmark says Porto something. Crikey, I think—'

'Not too loud, dear,' his mother said in an undertone, and made a movement of her head in Philippa's direction. All day she had been trying to tone Leslie down. But it was a pretty hopeless task.

What was that manuscript thing among Elizabeth Rusman's belongings? Philippa thought. How did it go? I did remember it for a time. The first notes were: E, C, D, E, G . . . F, E, D, E, C . . .

She tried this out on the piano, adding simple harmonics, and soon remembered how it went.

Leslie, full of philatelic zest, hesitated a moment now that Aunt Philippa was playing again. Then he touched his father on the arm.

'The postmark says Porto Rico, Dad. Where's that?'

'Er—' John looked up again. 'In South America too.'

'Yes, but what part of South America?'

'I thought you were good at geography,' John said. 'You tell me.'

This was too much for Leslie. 'You don't know!' he exclaimed in delight. 'Mummy, Daddy doesn't know where Porto Rico is! Isn't that great!'

John laughed good temperedly. 'Get the atlas and we'll look it up.'

They looked it up.

Philippa rose from the piano and went to the window and lit a cigarette. The glass was streaming with the rain. The dark drooping greenness out of doors suited her mood.

She was full of harrowing afterthoughts about the trial, being sure now that she might have found something more to say which might have helped to influence the jury. She had expected a much longer ordeal in the box; but Wells had seemed to want to cut it as short as possible. And she was worried too about the judge's question to her. 'You ask us to believe,' he had begun, as if he did not believe himself. Did that mean the judge was against them?

' "Porto Rico," ' read Leslie. ' "A West Indian island lying seventy-five miles east of Haiti." Where's Haiti, Daddy?'

'A West Indian island,' said John, 'seventy-five miles west of Porto Rico.'

Leslie looked mischievously at his father. 'Anyway, it isn't in South America.'

Silence fell, while the rain continued to run down the glass. Leslie flipped over the pages of his album and whistled under his breath.

Suddenly Philippa turned and stared across the room, the cigarette smouldering in her hand. Then in a flash she was across the room and standing opposite the boy.

143

For a few seconds Leslie was unaware of the move.

'Porto, Porto, Porto, Porter, Porter, Po-po-po-po . . .'
he went on.

Joan Newcombe, alarmed, stood up.

'Philippa . . .'

'*Leslie*' said Philippa.

Leslie jumped. 'What?'

'Philippa, dear, is he annoying you?'

'Leslie!' said Philippa. 'What's that you were whistling?
What is it you were whistling? Tell me.'

'Um?' said Leslie, frightened by the look on her face
and getting up. 'What's what, Aunt Philippa?'

'Was it the whistling that upset you?'

Her face white to the lips, Philippa turned to Joan.

'*Please*, Joan. Just a minute . . . That tune, Leslie.
Where did you hear it? Tell me, please. Where did you
hear it?'

Leslie stared. 'Which one? I don't know what you
mean.'

John too was on his feet, but Philippa ran past him to
the piano.

'This one,' she said.

After a few moments Leslie's face cleared. 'Why, you'd
just played it, Aunt Philippa. That's why I whistled it.'

'Yes, but where did you hear it before? You couldn't
have whistled it straight off after me if you hadn't heard it
somewhere before!'

Leslie frowned. 'I – I don't remember. Why?'

'It sounds a very ordinary little tune,' John said.
'What's all the fuss about, Philippa?'

'Just for a minute please,' she said, 'try not to interrupt
us. It's desperately important. Listen while I play it.'

There was silence at last while she played it again.

'It sounds like a hymn,' Joan said.

'Leslie . . .'

Reassured now that he had not committed some awful sin, Leslie put his wits to work.

'Ye-es,' he said. 'I remember it now. It's the tune Bungey Baker had on the brain in the Christmas hols. He kept on whistling it till I got it too.'

'Who is Bungey Baker?'

'Don't you know Bungey Baker?' Leslie asked in surprise. 'I thought everyone knew Bungey Baker. *He's* one of those chaps who seem to know everybody. . . .'

'He's a boy Leslie met on his holidays last year and they struck up a friendship,' Joan said. 'He spent Christmas with us. Philippa, I wish you'd explain—'

'Where does he live?' Philippa asked the boy. 'Have you his address?'

Leslie frowned. 'It's in Hampstead. I can't remember where, but I can get it you in a jiff. He lent me a book, and I've got it upstairs. Would you like me to fetch it now?'

'Please, Leslie.'

The boy ran off.

And then Philippa explained.

For a few minutes they were irritatingly slow to see the significance of the facts, irritatingly anxious that she should not build too much on it.

'I know that,' she said. 'I know it may lead to nothing. But don't you see I've got to follow it. I've got to see the boy Baker tonight and find out where he learned that tune. He must have heard it a lot somewhere, and it's the fact that it was in manuscript in Elizabeth Rusman's case which makes it so important. I did try one or two music shops and none of them knew it. You see, if it was printed, why should she bother to copy it in manuscript form?'

They couldn't answer her, although they were only half convinced. She had done so much this last month,

Swindon, Bournemouth, Canterbury, Utrecht, extravagant quests that had led nowhere. Did this mean another one right in the middle of the trial?

Leslie came scooting down.

'Here you are, Aunt Phil,' he said, and displayed a book on the flyleaf of which was written in a spidery round hand. '*This Book is the Property of: Benjamin Henry Baker, 260 West Terrace, Hampstead, London, England, The World.*'

Chapter Eighteen

JOHN DROVE HER there in the pouring rain. Joan would have liked to come too, but she didn't want Leslie out till all hours, so she stayed behind with him.

They reached the centre of London in time for the early theatre traffic and nosed patiently through until they were in Regent's Park. Then in a few minutes they reached Hampstead and began to inquire for West Terrace. Twice they were wrongly directed, and eventually found the Bakers' house only to be told that Benjamin and his mother had just gone to the pictures. . . .

The maid said she did not know which cinema they had gone to, and Mr Baker was not yet home. She did not ask them in, so they went back and sat in the car while the rain trickled down the windscreen. There are few things harder to bear with patience than being bent with desperate urgency on some course and being balked by life set in its commonplace routine. Nothing moved out of the normal rut to make way for the abnormal. Mrs Baker and Mr Benjamin had gone to the pictures and would not be back till nine. Mr Baker was out and had given no time for his return. John Newcombe looked at his companion's gloved hands endlessly fingering her bag, and drove her off to a restaurant for some food and drink to pass the time of waiting. . . .

At eight they went back again and this time found Mr Baker at home. They introduced themselves and explained their visit. There was no piano, so Philippa was forced to hum the tune. Mr Baker looked self-conscious and rubbed his nose and said he didn't know it, though, now he came to think, he believed he had heard Benjamin whistling something like that.

'I'm afraid I don't quite understand what the – er – the importance of this tune is to you, Mrs Talbot; but I'm sure Benjamin will be glad to help in any way he can. Would you care to wait till he comes home?'

They would care to wait.

Mr Baker turned on the electric fire and the radio and excused himself, and from then until nine-fifteen, a time that seemed like a century, Philippa smoked endless cigarettes and listened despairingly to Saturday Night Music Hall and the Nine O'clock News.

At last they heard voices in the hall, and Philippa could imagine the whispered conversation that was going on. 'My dear, two *extraordinary* people ... Some *tune* ... Newcombe ... Yes, where Benjamin stayed ... It's connected with that trial. You *know* Talbot is Newcombe's brother-in-law ... I don't know ... They attach some curious importance ...'

The door opened and a woman in a fur coat stood there. With her was a plump boy with spectacles awry and the chubbiest, cheeriest face Philippa had ever seen. She knew at once that he would enjoy this.

Once again, with Henry Baker stroking his nose and hovering curiously in the background, she had to tell them enough to explain the visit, and then at once she began to hum the tune. Bungey Baker's twinkling eyes were bright behind his spectacles.

'Oh, yes,' he said before Philippa had finished. 'I know that all right. I suppose I did have it on the brain a bit last Christmas. We had it drummed into us a bit at breaking-up time ... and it's got a sort of catchy air, hasn't it?'

'Where did you hear it?'

'At school. At my prep. school. I've left there now. I left at Christmas—'

'Now that we've moved to the south of England it was too far for Benjamin to travel,' said Mrs Baker. 'Every term. A day's journey.'

'What's the name of the school?' Philippa asked.

'Penmair. That's the name of the village too. It's in Scotland.'

'About thirty miles from Edinburgh,' supplied Mr Baker.

'Did you use this tune for anything particular?' Philippa asked the boy.

'Yes, it was our breaking-up song. Every school has one, you know.'

'I haven't heard this one before. Is it a special one for your school?'

'Oh, yes, it's quite new,' said Bungey. 'I think someone wrote it at the school.'

Philippa's heart began to thump.

'Had you any mistresses at the school, Bungey?'

'Oh, yes ... there were two. An arts mistress and a music mistress.'

'What was the music mistress like to look at?'

This was rather too much for Bungey. He pushed up his lop-sided spectacles. 'What, Miss Wharton? Oh, she was all right.'

'What age would she be?'

'Oh ... pretty old.'

'About thirty?' suggested Philippa.

'Yes, I should think about that.'

'Was she very dark with a good skin and large brown eyes and played the violin?'

Bungey was thoughtful. 'Yes, that'd be her. She was bad-tempered sometimes.'

Philippa stood up.

'Thank you, Bungey. You've been most helpful.'

'Has he really?' said Mrs Baker, gratified. 'You're Miss Shelley, the opera singer, aren't you? I recognized you from your photos in the paper We do hope what Benjamin has told you will be of real value to you. . . .'

So do I, thought Philippa, as she stuffed a few things into her bag at the flat. So do I. And I really believe he has. This time I'm really off. A music teacher at a school. Why didn't any of us think of that before? Don't get too excited yet; it may still come to nothing.

John, at the telephone and watching her hasty packing, decided to make one last attempt.

'Look, my dear, why not let the police break their hearts over this? It's been pretty clever of you ferreting out the thing; but with the suspicion now thrown on Mike Grieve it won't help the defence all that much to fill in the missing years. Nobody's suggesting Mike Grieve knew her before, and it's not necessary to suggest it. The best thing would be to see Archer and tell him what you think. Then instead of your having to go racing off to Scotland he would put through a telephone-call and the local police would check up in a few hours.'

Curiously, John could not have chosen his phrases better to strengthen her intent. There rose to her mind the picture of a policeman with bicycle clips making slow clumsy inquiries at the school. A distorted picture of course. But . . .

John said: 'It may mean your missing the last day of the trial and perhaps will cause you endless trouble only to meet another dead end. With time so short it should be out of our hands now.'

'I can be back on tomorrow night's train,' she said,

staring into her bag. This was a completely blind move and she could not tell whether there might be something she would specially want. She would take night things in case something delayed her and she did not catch to-morrow night's train. But she must or she would miss the trial. Nick would wonder . . .

John was speaking on the telephone now. After a few moments he hung up.

'The night express leaves at ten-fifteen. They've no sleepers left, but there may be a seat.'

She glanced at her watch. It was going to be a close call. She ran to a side table and scribbled a note.

'If I shouldn't be back early on Monday, John, will you see Nick gets this. I want him to know why I'm away.'

'Right.'

Twenty-five minutes before the train went. She glanced round the flat. When she saw this again . . .

They went out, and the car slipped along towards King's Cross.

There was a queue at the booking office and only three minutes remained to go as she hurried up the platform. Doors were already banging.

'Here we are,' said John, opening a carriage in which there was a seat.

She got in breathlessly as a whistle sounded and was echoed down the farther length of the train.

He looked at her. He was a Philistine where opera was concerned and at one time had been inclined to look with comical dismay on having an opera singer as a sister-in-law. But six weeks of fairly close acquaintance had converted him so far as this one was concerned.

'Good luck, Philippa,' he said, taking off his hat as the train began to move. 'You deserve it.'

Chapter Nineteen

HOURS OF SITTING upright, wanting to stretch and hardly able to, or dozing in half-cold half-humid stuffy darkness while the great train drew away through the swirling smoky glooms of the night. Then hours more it seemed while the darkness became grey and faded into a tattered dawn like an unwashed shirt, and nondescript hills creeping past. She had never felt train-sick in her life, but there was the beginning of a sick headache somewhere before Edinburgh was reached.

It was raining in Edinburgh when she got out, but for a moment this was unimportant beside the need for hot tea. She drank two cups at a refreshment-room, nearly scalding her mouth. At one time she would have been careful for her throat, but now that didn't seem to matter.

Presently she went out into the station again and stopped a porter.

She said: 'Can you tell me, please, when I can get a train to Penmair?'

The porter looked at her. 'Do you mean Penmair by the sea or Loch Penmair, leddy?'

'I think it's by the sea.'

'Oh, then you do mean Penmair. You'll no get a connection for Penmair the day. They have no trains there on a Sunday. Nor have they trains for Loch Penmair either,' he added as a helpful afterthought.

'Do you know where I can hire a car?'

'You could try on the rank outside, leddy. You might find one who could take you that far.'

She thanked him and went out into the rain. John had

been able to lend her the contents of his pocket-book, so she had plenty of available money.

She walked past the ordinary town taxis and went up to a grey-haired man who looked as if he owned his own cab. The man was agreeable, stating his price beforehand, and they set off. The sky was lighter now and after a while the rain stopped.

Although they had said it was only thirty miles, the morning was well on before she glimpsed the sea.

'Where in Penmair did you want to go?' he asked.

'Is there a hotel where I could put up?'

'Yes, yes. Where the parents stay when they come to visit their boys.'

'Can we see the school yet?'

'In a moment. Now, over there, beyond the village, on the headland. D'you see?'

Philippa stared. 'Yes, I see . . . I suppose it's all closed up now?'

'That I don't know, ma'am. I've no idea whether the boys are back yet.'

After a few minutes they bumped over a stone bridge spanning a stream and purred in a dignified fashion down the main street of Penmair.

It was a straggling village, with grey stone cottages, a gaping garage, four or five shops and the hotel. Farther along were a few houses and beyond them a dozen modern bungalows. The road climbed through a copse of firs to the school buildings on the hill. What have I come here for? she thought, and what can I do now I'm here? Wasn't John perhaps right? There's so little time.

She got off at the hotel and paid the driver, watched the car begin its journey back to Edinburgh. Then she went in and booked a room. It would give her a foothold in the place even though she did not intend to stay the night.

When it came to signing her name she hesitated briefly and wrote '*Joan Newcombe*'. She regretted now having brought no old clothes which might help to hide her rather obvious identity. The only thing she had with her was a pair of plain glass spectacles, worn once in a light opera. She put them on.

At the reception-desk she said: 'Is the school open yet?'

'No. The new term begins next Friday.'

'Well, will there be someone in charge? I came about sending my son.'

'I b'lieve Mr Fleming's at home. And of course there's the por-rter.'

'Mr Fleming?'

'Yes. The headmaster. Ye havena an appointment?'

'No. I came unexpectedly. Er – do you know if the violin is taught? My son is very musical.'

'Oh, aye; everything is taught, you may be sure.' The manageress was not interested. 'But Mr Fleming will tell you all that.'

'As a matter of fact,' Philippa said, 'I did know one of the women teachers at the school. I don't know if she is still there. A Miss Wharton.'

'Oh . . . Miss Wharton,' said the manageress, adding up her books. 'Yes, that's the dominie's daughter. Yes. I b'lieve she does teach music there.'

'Is she still at the school?' Philippa asked quickly. This was the first real stroke of luck she had met with in all her searches.

'Pardon? . . . Oh, no. She won't be there now.'

'Why? . . . What happened to her?'

The manageress looked up. 'Happened to her? Why, nothing, except that she is still on holiday. If you want to see her the best thing is to call in at her father's house. It's down the village. The house past the council school.'

Chapter Twenty

PHILIPPA WAS OUT in the street again. The puddles were smaller and the slates drying. A very cold, very fresh wind blew.

She didn't know where she was now. All her bright ideas had come toppling down. A school and a hymn tune and a music mistress about thirty with dark hair and brown eyes. It all seemed so very obviously linked up. Where had her mind imagined a link which was not there? She began to walk down the street.

She passed the squat little council school with its railings and its flagged playground, and turned up towards the next house which had a greenhouse and lace curtains. She rang the bell and a tall bony young woman came to the door. Philippa's heart sank, for she saw the mistake now. She answered the description given to Bungey Baker, but anyone less like Elizabeth Rusman would have been hard to find.

'Miss Wharton?'

'Yes.'

Philippa did her best to smile.

'I'm sorry; I've made a mistake, but I was calling at the school and someone said a Miss Wharton taught music there, and I wondered if it was the Mary Wharton I went to school with in Edinburgh.'

Miss Wharton said: 'My name's Harriet Wharton. Sorry.'

'You do teach the violin at Penmair, don't you?'

'I teach music generally but chiefly the piano.'

'Is there anyone else there who teaches the violin? I'm most anxious that my son should learn.'

'No, but I can start boys off in the right way. In the early stages, you know, it's very much a question of learning how to hold the fiddle properly and build up the notes. I've done all that side of it, even though I don't play much myself.'

They talked for some minutes and then Philippa withdrew. The dead end that John had feared? Not yet. Not quite yet. Feeling miserably tired and despondent, she closed the iron gate and began to walk up towards Penmair.

There were four buildings altogether: the big central one with what looked like a chapel attached, two smaller houses and a kind of converted porter's lodge beside open gates.

She went in and saw a man coming slowly towards her. He was distinctive in grey and red, with grey hair and a shiny magenta face to match.

She said: 'Good morning. I'd like to see the headmaster, please.'

The old man said: 'I doubt he's in, ma'am. It's his custom to attend divine sar-vice of a Sunday morning and when the school chapel's no in use he goes down to the village.' Slowly, as if the movement were an effort, he turned his head. 'I havena seen him go today, but . . .'

'I wanted to see him about sending my son as a pupil to the school.'

'Well, that's where he lives, ma'am.' The Scotsman pointed to the smallest of the three buildings. 'If ye've the mind to go up and knock. I havena seen him leave, though I expect he'll have gone.'

'Thank you,' said Philippa, and walked on.

She reached the house. These three buildings really

made up three sides of a square, the open side facing the village. She lifted the brass knocker on the green wooden door, noticing that the metal was considerably tarnished. No doubt the sea air.

She waited. A seagull flickered over the roof tops and cried. She knocked again.

She tried to picture these buildings as they would be in term-time, buzzing with life. Ninety or a hundred Bungey Bakers . . . 'Someone wrote it at the school . . .' Would all his information prove as delusive as that about the music mistress?

She knocked a third time and then on a sudden impulse tried the handle. The door opened and she stepped inside.

It was really the silence that had done it. One got the feeling that there could be nobody for miles and miles. Mr Fleming would be at divine sar-vice. But what of a wife or housekeeper?

She stared at the grandfather's clock in the hall. Courting trouble of the worst kind. 'Well, of course, I knocked three times and thought you hadn't heard.' 'My dear, she *said* she'd come about her son, but really I believe she was after the silver.' Get out, Philippa, before you make a fool of yourself.

Stairs and a door. She tried the door. It wasn't recklessness that sent her on but sheer desperation. So much to do, so little time to do it. Who'd said that?

A room like any other room. Stained floor, rugs, leather chairs, a grand piano – ah!—, framed Botticelli prints, a few photos, another door. She took a step forward.

A shadow moved ahead of her, and she realized the sun had come out. Pleasant room facing south. Had Elizabeth Rusman ever been in here? Looking out on a green

quadrangle as she did now. A seagull cried: *ya-ya-ya*.
Boys' feet on the turf. . . .

She went across and stared at the photo on the piano.
Two young men in flannels. On the mantelpiece was a
cricketing eleven.

The room was *dusty*; she'd just realized that: dusty and
cold. And the windows needed opening. She thought she
heard a creak behind her and swung round in alarm, but
there was nothing.

That farther door. Leave well alone. Go while the going
was good. . . . She tiptoed across and opened the door
and looked into a kitchen. This was untidier than the
other room. Plates and cutlery were piled in the sink, and
a primus stove, which had evidently done most of the
recent cooking, stood in the middle of the floor with a
paraffin can and a bottle of methylated spirits beside it.

Suddenly, in the hall through which she had come, the
clock began to strike midday. . . .

She stood there frozen until it had finished and then
with the fear of discovery, which had been clamouring
away all this time, now too strong to withstand, she
turned sharply, closing the door, to tiptoe in haste back
across the living-room. It seemed that instead of silence
the house was full of creaks and half-formed footsteps
and breaths of wind.

She ran across the hall and slid out of the front
door. . . .

Conscious of enormity and the peering eyes of fifty
windows, she walked back across the green and past the
lodge.

The old man put his head out. 'Did ye see Mr Fleming?'

'No. There was no one in.'

'Aye, he's at church. I thought he would be.' The
matter thus settled, the head withdrew.

Philippa walked back to the village, the wind pushing at her shoulder and flapping her skirts. Hope springs eternal, she thought. Well, it had sprung frequently enough in her, but now the mechanism was beginning to run down. Even if there was any clue to be found here – and even if by some miracle it was a clue which would help in Nick's defence – the time was now too short. The schoolmasters were scattered on vacation; any one of ten or fifteen might have known Elizabeth slightly during the war years and have brought the song to the school – or given the manuscript music to Elizabeth; or she might have got it in a dozen other ways.

Well, she'd done her best: backwards and forwards about the country and in London and Holland, asking, asking, asking, meeting the suspicious stare, the curiosity, the open rebuff. As a girl she had sometimes taken part in house to house collections for charity, but had always disliked them because a single refusal made her feel impertinent and interfering. During the quests of this last month all these old dislikes and timidities had come up and had had to be faced and overcome in intensified form. That she had overcome them had been a measure of her determination. But she was coming to the end now.

As she reached the main street a good many more people were about and she realized they were just coming out of church. She glanced at the first comers, but receiving back their curious stares, she dropped her eyes and turned to look in a shop window. It was the only shop that hadn't got its blinds down, but some of the groceries had been taken out of it and she found that the mirror at the side reflected most of the street to her view.

She wondered what Nick was doing. Usually he went to chapel on a Sunday morning at Brixton and then spent the afternoon reading. How many more hours would he have to spend in the witness-box tomorrow? Brooke Bond's tea, Knight's Castile soap. An old man passing in a donkey cart: *he* hadn't been to church. What were the jury doing? she wondered. Would they be kept together or allowed to disperse to their own homes?

Quite suddenly her attention stiffened as if someone had struck her. Passing up the street was a woman between two men. And one of the men might have been Nick. . . .

She swung round and stared after them. The resemblance was gone now. It had been a chance mistake, something in the angle of the mirror and a likeness of build. Why had it struck her? Perhaps she needed food. She had had no breakfast, practically nothing to eat for eighteen hours. Oh, she was going crazy; soon she would see Elizabeth Rusman coming out of one of the houses. It was the strain, the disappointment, the endless frustration. And yet . . .

On impulse she turned and walked quickly after them. They had got well ahead by now and were moving in the direction of the last houses, climbing the rising ground near the clump of firs. Presently they halted before a house with a brass name-plate. So they were stopping short of the school.

She found she had no excuse to dawdle but must go past them. As she did so she heard the lady say to the taller of the men – the one she had seen:

'I'm surprised to hear you quote the Jesuits. I'm sure it's not a nice thing to do after coming to church with us.'

The man gave a short laugh. 'Misquote them probably, Mrs Wishart. I never remember whether it is five or seven years they specify. But I'm concerned with the later years . . .'

She was past and walked on as far as the fir coppice. There she waited.

As if this was something deeper than knowledge, as if some sort of intuition was warning her that this time she wasn't crying wolf in vain, she was not surprised to see the tall man coming on alone.

He was about the same build as Nick but older, with, she thought, greying hair. As he came up she saw there was really no resemblance at all.

He glanced curiously at her and would have passed on, but she said:

'Forgive me. Are you Mr Fleming?'

'I am,' he said, and as he looked at her with his light brown gaze it was as if there was a flicker of puzzled recognition in *his* eyes.

'I'm Mrs Newcombe,' she said. 'I called at the school but you were out. I wanted to see you about sending my son to the school.'

He inclined his head. 'I'm so sorry. Perhaps you'll be able to call again?'

'I should like to,' she said. 'But I have to go back to London tomorrow. I was wondering if you could see me later today?'

'I have an engagement this afternoon. Would six this evening be convenient?'

'Thank you. That will do very well.'

He raised his hat and they parted.

Where have I seen her? he thought. I connect her with something, perhaps it's a likeness; I mustn't get suspicious of everyone. Why did I talk about an engagement this afternoon? It's the practice of lying that grows. Or is it that I now shirk new contacts? Putting off. She reminds me of someone. Perhaps by this evening I shall know.

He's not like Nick, Philippa thought, except in build and general features. But would it be enough for Grieve to mistake? He's not like Nick except now and then: that sudden crinkling of the eyes. They might be distant cousins.

She got back to the hotel and realized she was nearly fainting with hunger. After a meal which contrived to be fairly satisfying, she found the manageress in a more talkative mood.

'Och, it's a good school,' she said. 'Your son'll be well looked after there, and the air is fine, makes 'em eat and makes 'em grow.'

'I met Mr Fleming this morning.'

'Yes, he's a good schoolmaster. And a god-fearing man too. A wee bit strict with the boys, they say. But no wonder, for you have to be wi' lads of that age.'

Philippa wondered if that remark would be likely to endear Mr Fleming to a prospective client.

'What was that?' she said.

'I said he was only here for another term, for he's been appointed to the headmastership of Lovell's in Glasgow. A big move up for him, but no doubt he deserves it.'

'Is he married?' Philippa asked.

'Oh, yes. . . . Mrs. Fleming is away staying with relations. If you want tea, just ring the bell, will you?'

'How long has she been away?' asked Philippa.

'Who?'

'Mrs Fleming.'

'Oh, a couple of months it'll be now – perhaps more. I think it was about the end of February.'

'I suppose that would be her photograph I saw in his sitting-room. A good-looking woman, younger than he is, very dark, rather sallow, with large eyes.'

'Yes,' said the manageress. Just 'yes', and went away.

The afternoon dragged on as if it would never end. Twice she went out and walked round the village, wondering if there was anything more she could do. Was this another blind alley she was entering? She felt it was not.

On her second outing she called at the garage and got the promise of a car into Edinburgh leaving Penmair at a quarter to nine. Once she thought of calling on the doctor she had seen talking to Fleming, but realized that without some authority she could never get anything out of him. At four-thirty she had tea and at five she went up to her bedroom, washed and put a little powder on her face but no lipstick. The spectacles were some use, she thought; but she wished she had a brimmed hat that would hide her face. At five-thirty she set herself to smoke one last cigarette before going out. At twenty to six she left the hotel.

The sky was heavy with cloud, which hung low over the expressionless sea. If it had not been for the birds singing one could have taken it for the early twilight of a winter's afternoon. Among the fir trees there were pools on the road and a dozen starlings were fluttering and splashing. They flew away in a cloud as she came up and chattered at her from the trees.

As she came near the gates of the school she saw a figure standing there. It was Fleming.

'I thought I would meet you,' he said quietly. 'I sent the porter off, and he isn't back yet.'

The clock in the tower was just striking six.

Chapter Twenty-one

HE LED HER straight across to the main school building, talking affably. She could not decide whether he was a Scot or not. There was no accent. She saw that he had charm when he wished to exert himself; it showed through the first impression of rather prosy dryness. Parents would think, how deceptive these schoolmasters are. Imagination, or a greater awareness, made Philippa keen to catch the undertones, and once or twice she sensed the insincerity behind the telling phrases. They had been repeated so often that they were worn smooth.

But they were the phrases designed to appeal to parent or guardian, designed perhaps to conceal a certain contempt for this side of schoolmastering; when he spoke of teaching a different note crept into his voice.

He unlocked the big door and stood aside for her to go in. She found herself in a large square hall with some framed oil-paintings and rows of hooks with only one scarf and raincoat left on them. It was not very light in here for the windows were high. She stared round and listened to him carefully relocking the door behind him. For a few seconds she stood quite still. Then he came up beside her.

'This way, please. We'll go out by the other door.'

They walked down the hall, their feet sounding hollow on the boards.

'Were you recommended, Mrs Newcombe?' he asked suddenly.

'Yes. The Henry Bakers. Their son Benjamin was here.'

He nodded. 'He left last year. An intelligent boy. But

he's the sort who may waste his talents – if he's allowed.'

They turned a corner and he opened another door.

'This is one of the classrooms.'

She stared at the desks, the blackboard with the white chalk marks blurring the outer edge. It was all desolate, cold and desolate.

'We specialize in small classes,' he said. 'I've made it a principle since I came here. Teaching should be a co-operation. Lectures are useless.'

'Are you musical, Mr Fleming?' she asked as they turned to go out.

'No.' His pale brown eyes met hers.

'I should like Leslie to take music, and I noticed—' She stopped. What incredible madness was going to make her mention the piano in his sitting-room. '—noticed that the Baker boy had a good grounding.'

He seemed for a moment to be watching her closely.

'Cantley is our choir-master, and Miss Wharton takes some classes. No doubt you saw their names in our prospectus.'

'I haven't had one,' she said. 'I was in Edinburgh on a family matter and came to see the school quite on the impulse of the moment.'

'You are staying at the hotel?'

'Not tonight. I'm hoping to catch the night train back to London.'

They were climbing the stairs now, he three steps behind her. They were wide stairs with carved banisters into which knobs had been screwed at intervals to spoil an obvious sport. He walked very quietly. When there was any carpet she could not hear his steps at all.

'Has this been an old manor house?' she asked.

'It was built by the family of Donald about a hundred years ago. They were a spendthrift lot. The place has never been put to such good use as now.' He opened another door. 'This is one of the dormitories.'

A blind flapped in the breeze. Little cubicles like little horse boxes stood open to the eye. She could picture them in their striped flannel pyjamas larking and giggling and sucking forbidden sweets.

'The senior boys are only two to a room.'

What did one say, what questions ask?

'Is there a prefect in each dormitory?'

'We don't have prefects in this school, Mrs Newcombe. It is the essence of the system I have instituted that I should trust the boys and they should trust me.'

'Do you find that works?'

'Certainly. It's no good bringing up children to do right because they're forced to. They must learn to do right by the example of others.'

He was leading the way along another passage. Was this humbug? she wondered. Every instinct told her it was not. If she was here as a genuine parent seeking a school for her son, would she be convinced that this was the man to educate him? She might well be. There was the stamp of sincerity on his words now. Yet did she believe this and at the same time suspect him of—

'This is the junior common-room. Behind the curtains at the end is a small stage where amateur dramatics are held in the winter term. It's a valuable form of self-expression. . . .'

She looked out of the window at the grey shimmer of the sea. It was dark, but the clouds were breaking. She looked round the big shadowy room with its bentwood chairs and its table-tennis and its dartboard. She glanced at the man standing in the doorway. His eyes were narrowed and again he was looking at her. If he recognizes me, she thought, what then?

'How old is your son?' he said.

She hesitated a moment.

'Eight.'

'Is he a good boy?'

'Well, I think so. Of course, he's so young.'

Fleming said: 'If you have led him rightly so far, we will lead him rightly here.'

Somehow she was glad to be out of that room with its tall grey walls. But here in the passage it was still darker. He put no light on. And was she getting any further in this quest? She suspected; but suspicion alone would not clear Nick. Suspicion she could have voiced in London.

'Where has he been until now?' the man following her asked.

'Oh, just to a little local school.' Philippa stopped at a branch in the passages so that he had to take the lead. 'Forgive me, Mr Fleming, are you married?'

'Yes – but my wife is abroad at the moment.' He half turned. 'Why do you ask?'

'Don't you find it lonely here after all the noise and bustle of term-time?'

'I like the quiet, Mrs Newcombe.'

She said: 'The manageress at the hotel told me you were leaving the school soon.'

'Yes.'

'I'm sorry.'

'I'm sorry too. But greater responsibility is what I want. Teaching's in my blood.' He went on.

They saw two other rooms almost in silence. It was a taut silence, as if something had been stretched between them during this last lap.

'Would you like to see the chapel?'

'Thank you.'

They turned off down a covered way, their footsteps

hollow in the sham Gothic passage. He pushed open a great oak door and with an effort she took a grip of herself and went ahead of him.

A gleam of watery sun had come out and the stained-glass window over the altar was fiery with colour.

'What a lovely building.'

'Isn't it.'

She walked slowly in, past the pews, looked up at the arch of the transept.

'*Deus est qui regit omnia,*' she read.

She had not heard him come up beside her. 'The school motto. There is a God who rules all things.'

Her hands were cold with a sudden resolve.

'Is the organ a good one? Might I try it?'

He did not reply, and she moved forward as far as the seat before glancing back.

'Certainly,' he said. 'You'll find the switch on your left.'

She sat on the seat. Oh, God, she thought, now for it. No, not yet, give me a minute to get confidence. The window was blood-red in the sudden sun.

She moved the switch and heard the hum of the electric blower. She began to play one of Bach's preludes, one her father had taught her in the village church years ago. How sweetly normal they seemed, that church, that tune. Near poverty perhaps, but sweet and sane. She glanced in the mirror and saw that she could see Fleming reflected standing on the chancel steps.

She finished the prelude and began to play the song that Elizabeth Rusman had written.

Chapter Twenty-two

WITH COLD FUMBLING hands and sweat on her fore-head she played it through to the end, while the stained-glass window burned in the evening sun. Then she looked in the mirror again and saw that Fleming had moved. She could no longer see him.

He's coming up behind me, she thought, in a minute his fingers on my throat. Elizabeth choked, choked to death . . .

As her back straightened her fingers went down on the keys and she played a chord. And another chord, auto-matically. These notes came not from the brain but from muscles long ago attuned. She felt sick and faint but his fingers were not there.

She got up . . . from the organ, turned.

Not forward, he had not gone forward but back, out of the glow of the window.

She heard her own voice say: 'Yes, a very good organ. . . . Thank you.'

She walked slowly down the chancel steps. She could not see his face very well, but he stood aside to let her lead the way towards the door.

I can't again, not turn my back on him again. . . .

His shadow flicked along the bench ends beside her.

He said: 'You play the organ very well, Mrs New-combe.'

She had reached the door and waited for him to open it. As he opened it she saw his face a little more clearly. It was completely expressionless. Not a muscle moved. But there was a faint dampness of the skin.

Back along that covered way. On one side were school photographs, groups, year by year. Hundreds of little white dots, row on row, entities, held for a moment, gone now, records for the school.

Half-way along Fleming said:

'Where did you hear that song?'

Somehow even to talk of it was better than the silence.

'The little Baker boy was humming it all through the Christmas holidays when he came to stay with us. I hope his memory was good.'

'Quite good.'

'It's your school song, isn't it?'

'Yes.'

'It's original, isn't it? I wonder who wrote it.'

'I'm afraid I don't know. Now, is there anything more I can tell you, Mrs Newcombe?'

Would they never get out in the open? She felt she could walk no farther.

'I don't think so. Thank you for giving me so much of your time.'

'Not at all.'

The door. He was opening the last of them. Outside the watery sun was still shining across the grass.

'I'll write to you when I get back to London,' she said.

'Please do.'

He was coming out with her.

'Don't bother to come to the gate,' she said. 'I'm afraid I've given you a lot of trouble already.'

'No, it's been a pleasure.'

Put out your hand. Out. With a smile.

He took it.

'Good-bye, Mrs Newcombe.'

'Good-bye. And thank you.'

She went off.

Why has there to be this grass, she thought, not gravel so that I could hear footsteps?

The drive at last. No pink friendly face at the lodge. By the gate she turned as if to get a final view of the school. The door was shut and he was gone. But gone where? She only knew that no power on earth – not even the hope of saving Nick – would have induced her to go back and enter that empty building again.

She turned and went down the road. With relief came sanity and self-criticism. What had she done? Nothing but walk over a school. What had been said? Nothing but what might have been expected. Had she then somehow imagined the whole of the undercurrent of tension which had seemed to exist?

Police officers were not concerned with feminine intuition. What had she to tell them? Enough to cause an inquiry to be made? If Elizabeth Rusman had married and lived here, then Fleming would be in a tight position; he would have to explain why he had not come forward, why he had lied about her being abroad. Was there a loophole? What sort of an alibi had he for the time of the murder?

But had she any proof yet that Elizabeth had been his wife? Anything to take back with her as tangible evidence to stop the case against Nick?

She found herself back in the village and went straight to the hotel. There was still an hour before the car was due to call.

And when he shut the door again he went back to the chapel.

He sat in the front pew and looked up at the stained-glass window from which nearly all the colour had now faded. He did not try to pray, but his thoughts went round and round in his head like robots at a fair. The dragons, the gargoyles, the angels, the leaping horses and the winged devils. Which one should he ride?

In this crisis his reason had been uppermost all the time; there had only been one moment of slipping, but he had quickly controlled it.

He was not sure yet if he had acted for the best; sometimes the impulse of the moment is the clearer guide. He did not know. She was catching the night train, she said. That would mean Murray's car. What time did it go dark? This damned daylight saving. The sun would set in about an hour; then the long twilight. But it was a heavy evening. The light would be failing by the time the car left.

It was not a pretty problem. One weighed the risks, the advantages, the possible flaws in any action or inaction. Reason it out. Consider it carefully.

After twenty minutes he left the chapel and went out to his own car.

She had left the hotel again, restless and unable to wait. Once she thought of calling on Harriet Wharton and telling her everything. She had looked a hard-headed, sensible woman. Even one friend in this village might make all the difference. But she shrank away from the awful difficulty of explaining, of trying to convince her that she was not a lunatic. Harriet Wharton would say what everyone would say: go to the local police. And if she did, the incredible explaining to them, their looks of astonishment, their side glances, their telephone calls. In all probability one of the first people they would ring up would be Sidney Fleming.

She walked down the street and tried to think over all

172

they had said together in the school. Had he betrayed himself in any way? Put herself in his place. If the song meant to him all that she thought it meant, then he surely must know that she knew. Might she not leave the next move to him?

The thought gave her an unexpected twist of alarm and she glanced quickly up and down the street. There was hardly anyone about. She looked in the shop windows, most of which reflected her own image in their blinds. '*Macpherson and Son, Grocers and Provision Merchants.*' That was the one she had looked in this morning. '*Angus Baird, Newsagent and Stationer. Hardware. Photographic Supplies.*'

She moved on and then stopped, turned back. Angus Baird was a Jack-of-all-trades. In the list of his accomplishments were the words '*School Photographer*'.

There flashed back into her mind the school groups on the walls of the covered way. Rows of anonymous faces. But as she recalled them she remembered also the little humps in the middle of each photograph where the rows curved upwards into the adults. Were there not women among them? Surely. And would not one be the headmaster's wife? . . .

She pressed her face against the glass of the shop and could just see behind the blind. There were photographs in the window, but none which looked like a school group. But the man would surely have some in stock. There would be a fairly steady sale for them.

She stepped back and looked at the closed shop. There were two windows overhead and at the side a little wicket gate. She tried the gate and went in.

Round the side was a vegetable patch, a chicken run, a few discouraged tulips.

There was no knocker to the door, so she used her

173

knuckles. She waited impatiently, then knocked again. Pray they were not all out for the evening, like the Bakers.

The door opened eight inches and a small grey man peered out. He looked like a grey elderly ferret, disturbed and suspicious.

'Aye?'

'Please forgive me for troubling you,' she said. 'You are Mr Baird, the school photographer, aren't you?'

'Aye.'

'I saw the notice,' she said apologetically. 'I specially wanted a photograph of my nephew who was in last year's group. I should be so very much obliged if you could sell me one.'

The small elderly face regarded her without change of expression.

'Aye . . . If ye come round in the morning the shop will be open and ye can see them in a proper manner.' The door closed an inch.

Philippa said anxiously: 'I'm leaving Penmair in a few minutes to catch the London express from Edinburgh. Otherwise I shouldn't have troubled you tonight. It's really most important that I should take a photograph back with me. Really important. Perhaps you'll let me explain . . .'

The door closed another inch, defensively against her move. 'The shop will be open at nine o'clock in the morning, but not until then.'

'Mr Baird, it's not just an ordinary purpose I want it for. Perhaps you'd stretch a point and sell me one tonight. I should be so deeply grateful—'

'I neither buy nor sell on the Sabbath day.'

'I don't mind what I pay,' said Philippa. 'I'll give you whatever you ask—'

'I have no interest in money,' said Mr Baird, 'until the morning.' And he shut the door.

'Listen, please! It's vitally important!' Almost in tears she used her fist on the panel. 'Open this door!'

There was no reply. For a few seconds she stared at it, anger and frustration choking her. She would cheerfully have picked up a brick and thrown it through the window. She could have kicked the toe off her shoe and the paint off the door. But the look in his eye discouraged her. He was the stuff of which inconvenient martyrs are made. There was no hope here.

At ten the manageress of the hotel was coming out of the bar when a man walked into the hall of the hotel and looked about him.

'Oh, good evening, Mr Fleming,' she said. 'Cold this evening, isn't it?'

He agreed. 'Er – Mrs Drummond, have you a Mrs Newcombe staying here?'

'Why, yes, we have. Did you want to see her? I b'lieve she's just gone to bed.'

'It doesn't matter. But I understood she was leaving tonight.'

'Well, so did we, sir. She paid her bill and ordered a car. But at the last minute she cancelled it and was minded to stay on.'

'Till the morning?'

'That's so. Till the morning. She's ordered the car now for a quarter to nine.'

'Did she give any reason for changing her plans?'

'No, sir. I think perhaps it was the journey she didn't fancy.'

'Thank you.' Fleming was turning to go.

'Can I give her some message, sir?'

'Er – no. It doesn't matter. But perhaps you'd give her this. It's a prospectus of the school. She forgot to take it earlier this evening.'

'Oh, all right, Mr Fleming. Thank you. Good night.'

'Good night, Mrs Drummond,' he said.

Chapter Twenty-three

SHE DREAMED STRANGE things in the night: that she was on trial for her life and Fleming was the prosecuting counsel, that the trial was being held in the empty school and that no one was there besides themselves. He stormed and shouted, but all his shouts were soundless and the only thing that came to her ears was the steady striking of the school clock.

The sound was so mournful echoing through the hollow shell of the school that she realized the trial was really over and that this was the tolling of the bell for the execution. She knew that the hanging was to take place in the chapel under the organ and that Fleming was to be the executioner. He was coming down from his rostrum now and holding out his hand. . . .

She woke cold and shivering to find that the eiderdown had slipped to the floor. Dawn was just breaking and there was no more sleep for her. She lay for a time wondering if she had been unwise in not telephoning home last night. It was really that she disliked having nothing tangible to tell them. The trial could not be over today unless it went on very late, and her train was due in at six. As soon as she had the proof she would phone or wire them.

At seven she got up, and she was dressed and ready to go before the maid brought in her early morning tea. She had breakfast and was waiting on the step when Murray drove up in his Austin 14.

She said: 'I want you to go to Baird's first, please. I've something I want to buy there.'

They drove to Baird's. It was still only twelve minutes to nine. They waited.

Murray said: 'I hope you'll not be long in buying what you want. It's a tidy way and not a road you can hasten over; and the Scotsman goes at ten.'

At five past nine Philippa got out of the car and tried the shop door. It was still locked, so she rattled it. She waited and then heard movements in the shop. Presently one of the blinds went up and she caught sight of a small grey wispy woman retreating into the interior of the shop like a mouse surprised by a light. Then the other blind went up, and a few moments later the bolt was drawn back from the door.

She went in.

They were both in there, one at each counter, but as she came in Baird himself went off out of the shop.

'May I see the school photographs, please,' she said to Mrs Baird. 'I want to see last year's specially.'

The little woman blinked at her.

'Aye. The school photographs. Aye . . . Angus!'

'Aye?' said a voice.

'Where would the school photographs be now?'

'Under the magazines. Behind the sweet bottles.'

'Aye.' The little woman shifted herself to the other end of the counter and began to fumble there. 'The new magazines, Angus?'

'No, the used ones.'

She shifted back again.

'Please hurry,' said Philippa. 'I have a train to catch.'

'Would these be they, Angus, in the grey album?'

'Aye.'

Mrs Baird slowly pulled out a thin album and spread it on the counter.

'Angus generally likes to sairve these himself,' she said.

Philippa pulled open the album and turned to the last filled page.

Her eyes flew to the middle of the group and to Fleming sitting very recognizable as the head. The woman beside him. . . .

The woman beside him. . . .

'I want to buy this,' said Philippa with a dry throat. 'How much is it?'

'Angus, how much would the photo be?'

'Two and sixpence.'

'Two and sixpence.'

Philippa brought out her money and watched in a sort of daze the new search for a print that could be sold. But for a few seconds the impatience had gone from her. All this time. All through the inquiries and troubles of yesterday the little devils of doubt had never been quite silenced. She had met so many, so very many dead ends, that all the time the thin thread of scepticism had lived in her most passionate convictions. This morning, with nothing to show for her adventure at the school yesterday, she had begun to wonder again if it was all a self-delusion.

Now she knew for certain it was not.

She was there, there on the print, sitting beside him, without hat, plain to be seen. Explain that, Mr Fleming.

Philippa thrust the rolled print into her bag and ran to the car. Triumph. Glorious triumph in her heart. Nick was safe, safe, whatever the outcome of the trial.

'I doubt we shall make it,' said Murray, slamming the door.

The car jerked into motion and accelerated harshly away down the street.

And into her heart, edging the joy about, a new anxiety and fear slowly crept. It was not so much a fear of missing the train, though that was bad enough. But she was hundreds of miles from London. An hour's drive by road, perhaps a wait in Edinburgh, then at least eight hours by train. All that time, until the photo was safely in the custody of the police, she was the bearer of Nick's safety. On her safety depended his safety.

And she was still afraid of Fleming.

When Murray started his engine it was a quarter-past nine, and his elderly car was not in a fit state for speeding. As they ground slowly up hills and careered recklessly down them he explained over his shoulder that he had a new car on order but couldn't get delivery. This didn't help Philippa.

Half-way there he glanced at the clock and then fumbled in the cubby-hole and passed her a railway time-table.

'We'll not make the Scotsman, but I think there's a later train. You'll find it all there.'

But how much later, she wondered, turning the pages helplessly for some time and then, in sheer desperation, forcing herself to understand the cross-references in the guide. There was, so far as she could make out, a slightly slower train leaving for London at ten-fifteen. It offered some hope.

At ten they were only on the outskirts of the city, and she began to wonder in panic if both trains would go without her. That would mean hours of waiting. At ten-past ten she pushed money into her driver's hand and ran into the gloom of the station.

'The Scotsman?' she cried to a porter.

'Gone, ma'am.'

'The next one? The ten-fifteen?'

'Over there. Just leaving. You'd best hurry.'

Hurry? What else was she doing? Faster than she had run for years she fled half the length of the station, turned in at the barrier and ran along the train. Whistle going. She opened a door and got in as the train whistled. Always last minute, she thought. But I've caught one of them. In London by seven now.

There were three people in the compartment, two middle-aged ladies sitting opposite her and an elderly man in the corner seat by the corridor. They were all interested in her breathless arrival. She put her case on the rack and sat down.

As always when a thing is put off, she thought, it never gets done. No telephone message, no wire. She might have time when the train stopped at York or somewhere: until then they would have no word of her in London. And all this day the trial would be going on without her.

She had been in too much of a hurry to notice Sidney Fleming sitting by the barrier at the station or to see him open a door and get into the back of the train.

As Nick stepped down from the witness-box he glanced at the empty seat beside Joan. Somehow, although he had complete faith in Philippa, he would have chosen that she should be here and have risked the loss of the possible evidence she might find in Scotland. He had had her note, but he wanted her presence today. It was nothing but her presence but he could not spare it.

The rest of the cross-examination had been long and gruelling. Wells had done his best to convict him out of his own mouth, and though he had not succeeded Nick understood its effect on the jury. He suspected that the average juryman, if overwhelmed with a sea of evidence, would pick on some salient fact and cling to it for the rest of the trial. There were several such facts, all adverse, in Wells's cross-examination.

Now Tyler was doing his best to destroy the effect.

'I believe, members of the jury, that the Crown made a mistake in ever bringing this case to trial. They expect us to believe that this old love affair was so dangerous to the married life of Nicolas Talbot that he went round to Miss Rusman's flat on the very night of their meeting and murdered her. That is the only motive. The Crown has not pretended to advance any other. If, in order to raise the intent to kill in a man's heart, no stronger compelling force than this was needed, murder would become a commonplace of life. I ask you frankly: if the existence of an old love affair were a sufficient motive for murder, *which of us here has not such a motive?*'

With his brilliant compelling eyes Tyler turned towards the court, seeming to include everyone in his question, before returning to the jury.

'Then they are asking us to believe that Talbot, wounded in the struggle, went immediately to the nearest hospital and asked for his wound to be dressed. Look at him in the dock! Look at him closely. If you can bring yourselves to believe that such a man would commit a brutal murder for so flimsy a reason, can you also believe that he would be so fantastically careless as to advertise his injury near the scene of the crime? I ask you first if he looks like a murderer, and second if he looks like a fool.'

Nick shifted under the scrutiny. Good logic, but change the angle, Tyler. I hate being held up like a prize cow.

'. . . Yes . . . we have his identification, a subject on which there are more *honest* mistakes made by witnesses than in any other evidence. *Honest* mistakes, mark you. Ask yourselves only who had most to gain by the identification of Nicolas Talbot? Who was the only man in the lodging house when Elizabeth Rusman came home? Who has already served a sentence in prison for assault on a

182

woman? Whom would the police have been most likely to suspect if Talbot had not been so unfortunately convenient to hand? The police have said that Mike Grieve could not have seen the locket after they arrived. I will not dispute their assertion. But no one, *no one alive,* can say that Mike Grieve couldn't have seen the locket *before* they arrived. . . .'

Philippa took the photo out of her handbag and stared at it. There was no mistake. No one could deny it. With every mile that the train rushed on, her confidence was returning, her fears subsiding. She rolled the photo into a thin roll and put it back in the handbag. She was glad she had done so, for at that moment the ticket collector came round.

The two ladies were the first to find their tickets, then Philippa. The elderly man in the corner was late in producing his, and when it came it was a return half from London to Berwick-on-Tweed, so extra had to be paid. He was quite prepared for this, but it was all complicated because he had to screw something into his ear and switch on a battery in his pocket before the necessary talk could even be carried on in shouts.

He beamed rather apologetically at the carriage, and his instrument went *crick-crick, crack-crack* for everyone to hear. Philippa wondered why some people thought deafness in others amusing; when as bad as this it was like a wall between a man and the rest of the world.

For the moment her thoughts had wandered from the trial and what she carried in her bag. Somehow she felt that she too was deaf, deaf in the spirit, not to hear, not to be able to *know*, what was going on at the Old Bailey when she so desperately needed and wanted to know. . . .

'Remember always that on your decision depends a

man's life,' Tyler was at that moment saying. 'You and only you can decide whether Nicolas Talbot shall die or whether he shall return to the woman who so passionately believes in his innocence. Remember that, before you can bring in a verdict of guilty, there must be no element of doubt in your hearts. You can take this man's life away from him but you can never restore it. If new facts come to light, as well they yet may, about Elizabeth Rusman's past life, you, each one of you, will bear the responsibility of having sent an innocent man to be hanged. I do not believe you will accept that responsibility. I believe that a verdict of "Not guilty" is the only possible verdict you can return.'

Nick glanced at Tyler as he sat down, knowing this was the final appeal. Nothing more could be said now. And, since the defence had called witnesses, the prosecution had the last word.

And Philippa had lunch, and the train stopped at Newcastle, and Mr Fleming got up from the very last compartment in the train and began to move along the corridor.

Chapter Twenty-four

'It should be emphasized,' Wells said, fingering the keys in his pocket, 'that it is no part of the Crown's intention to obtain a conviction at all costs. If the defence has made out a case which raises an element of doubt in your minds, then you, the jury, are in duty bound to return a verdict of not guilty. But . . . if the defence has *not* been able to produce facts to shake the evidence of the prosecution, then you are just as truly bound as responsible citizens to find the prisoner guilty – and no *merely emotional* appeals should be allowed to sway your judgement.'

Nick tore a sheet off his pad and began to write a note:

'Dear Joan, Where is Philippa? I can't understand her not being here yet or not even having sent a message. Can anything have happened to her? Something must be done . . .'

'The defence has asked you,' Wells said, 'if the prisoner looks like a murderer or a fool. What you should ask yourselves is not that, but whether in certain adverse circumstance he might not become a murderer and whether under stress following a crime he could not behave like a fool. The Crown does not ask you to imagine the prisoner as having cold-bloodedly planned his crime. We think it happened in passion and heat. Murder, when it occurs, is unnerving beyond my power to describe. Under the stress of such an event a man is not himself; he does not think calmly or act wisely.'

(And what, Sidney Fleming might have asked two hundred and fifty miles away, what when you have lived with the thought for six weeks and believed yourself safe, and another woman comes between you and safety and one woman only, her life or yours, do you think coherently or act wisely then; and wherein lies wisdom, to wait or to act?)

'Remember,' said Wells, 'the murderer thought the evidence was being destroyed by fire. It was not therefore so foolish a move to get his wound dressed before any description was circulated, before the hue and cry began. Remember that but for Mike Grieve's prompt action there might have been no hue and cry at all.

'As for this strange and ill-conceived attempt to throw suspicion upon another man, this is not the place to discuss it at length. But do you seriously think that the police would not have covered such a possibility, if such a possibility had in fact existed. I will only ask you one question. If Grieve had committed this murder and had *not* seen Talbot coming out of the lodging house, how was he able *exactly* to describe an injury he had never seen, *an injury by which Talbot was first recognized and apprehended*? *Nothing*, members of the jury, *nothing* the defence can say can lay the suspicion upon Grieve because of that.

'We have been told too that no man would commit murder to rid himself of the tiresome attentions of a discarded mistress. Who, then, would believe that Seddon the poisoner, a man in comfortable circumstances, would commit murder for a mere thirty shillings a week? Just for a moment consider again the case of Nicolas Talbot: a charming adventurer, spendthrift, pleasure-loving, indolent, for the first time in his life secure, financially secure in the love of a beautiful and talented woman . . .'

During the luncheon break Nick had asked Frobisher if the trial was likely to be over today, and Frobisher had said:

'It depends very much on Wells. If he finishes his closing speech before three Mr Justice Ferguson will probably sum up at once and keep the court in session until the jury reaches its verdict.'

Nick now looked at the clock and saw that it was only twenty-five minutes to three, and he could tell Wells was near the end.

'Members of the jury, the facts speak for themselves. A woman is murdered. Two hours before her death she has paid most unwelcome attentions to an old lover who stands to lose much by her reappearance, and she has forced an assignment upon him. Five minutes after her death a man is seen leaving her lodgings with a wounded forehead. Half an hour later a man is picked up with an *identical* wound at a neighbouring hospital and proves to be the lover with whom she made the appointment. Further, he can offer no alibi for his movements and his silver pencil is found beside the body. Then he is positively identified by the man who saw the murderer leave. Old love letters from Talbot and a locket with his photograph are found on the body. These are *facts,* members of the jury, *facts*; and the defence has not been able to destroy one of them. Short of an actual witnessing of the crime, what more could you have? The whole picture is there. I do not ask for revenge, but I do ask for justice, a justice which you are bound before God to uphold. And justice demands that Nicolas Talbot should be brought in *guilty.*'

He sat down at a quarter to three, and five minutes later the train drew in at York.

Amid the bustle of the two ladies getting out, Philippa left her coat on her seat and ran along the platform. There was a newspaper kiosk opposite the restaurant car, and she looked eagerly about it as other people were served.

'Have you an evening paper, please?' she asked.

187

'They're not in yet. Sorry.'

'Oh,' she said in disappointment, and did not move.

'You might get one on the main platform by the booking office.'

'Thank you.'

She looked at the clock. There was at least five minutes yet.

She ran up the steps and over the bridge, and at this larger book kiosk she was able to buy the local evening paper.

Not that it was likely to be much use, she thought, as she fled back. Would it even mention the case?

She reached her carriage, which she had some difficulty at first in finding, for both the deaf man and the two ladies were gone and a strange man sat opposite her seat, with his nose buried in *The Times*.

She sat down rather breathlessly and quickly scanned the paper she had bought. As she found the brief item the train began to move again.

It told her practically nothing. The cross-examination had been continued this morning with questions as to the exact movements of the accused man on the night of the murder.

She read it through again, and in frustration and disappointment put the paper down and stared out at the disappearing suburbs of the city.

Then she looked at the man opposite.

As if aware that she was now interesting herself in him, he lowered his paper.

'I didn't recognize you until you played the organ, Mrs Talbot,' he said.

Chapter Twenty-five

SOMEHOW SHE HAD known in the very marrow of her bones that it wouldn't be all quite so easy as it seemed. Her reason had said, 'Good, he can do nothing; Nick is saved and he will hang'; but instinct had all the time been sending out its warning signals. When she shook hands with him as she left the school she had sensed that he would not tamely give in.

Now at this moment the train was gathering speed out of the suburbs of York, and instead of his being shivering, waiting for the arrival of the police in his school at Penmair, he was sitting opposite her here, and if there was a tremor moving through his body from time to time it was not fear.

Slowly the shock began to pass out of her body, muscles moved again and heart beat. His eyes . . .

'How did you trace her?' he said.

She did not reply. The communication cord. But she must not look at it.

'Don't move,' he said. 'How did you trace her?'

She licked her lips, tried to speak.

'The way others will trace her in time.'

He was eyeing her, assessing the truth of what she said. And every few seconds his glance would flick to the corridor and then out of the window. He's waiting for something, she thought.

'You'd never reach it,' he said, as she glanced involuntarily upwards.

And suddenly she knew what he was waiting for. The

embankments were mounting up beside the windows. A tunnel coming now . . . This was what—

She saw the muscles tense in his hands as the train screamed. She had no breath. He was coming . . .

And then the door of the compartment clicked. The deaf man had come back as they roared into the tunnel.

Like effigies they faced each other across the narrow carriage, while the man in the other corner took a paper off the rack and settled himself in his seat. In the unreal pallid light of the lamps she could see Fleming's eyes still fixed on her.

With a rush they were out in the open again, rain spots spattering the window. In the clearer light she could see that only great self-control had held his intention in check: even with the man there it had nearly happened. Slowly he was forcing his body into an easier attitude.

The deaf man looked across at them.

'I've been to inquire what time they serve teas,' he volunteered. 'They begin in a quarter of an hour.'

Philippa looked at her deliverer.

'Oh . . .'

There was silence for a moment. Then the man turned his head again.

'Did you say something?'

Philippa shook her head. 'No. I . . .'

He glanced from one to the other of them, and his gaze lingered curiously for a moment on Fleming. He half smiled at Philippa.

'It's a great handicap, you know,' he said apologetically as he picked up the paper.

Fleming was watching him very closely. After a few seconds he said in a clear voice:

'Which way is the restaurant car?'

There was silence.

Fleming said loudly: 'Which – way – is – the – restaurant – car?'

The man in the corner turned over his paper and began to read the Stock Exchange closing prices.

Fleming's eyes turned back to Philippa. The light brown pupils were intent and personal and comprehending. He put his hands on his knees and looked at her.

It had come to her in these last moments that the deaf man's presence was only a respite. Fleming was capable of anything as a last resort. She must fight him if she wanted to live: first with her mind and then perhaps with her hands.

She said: 'You killed her, didn't you?'

Fleming said: 'Well, she left me, you know.' It was a quiet, reasonable, almost confidential answer. They might have been talking of a friend's visit.

'Why?' she asked.

He hesitated, the first sign of hesitation, and a curious expression crossed his face. He leaned forward.

'She was a fool . . . crying for the moon. . . .'

They rattled over a bridge and rushed alongside a broad stream. The rain was setting in steadily now. A woman passed along the corridor.

And then suddenly it came. He could not resist it; there was plenty of time and he must wait; let her know, this woman, who soon must follow Elizabeth, or he would follow.

'She was going to divorce me for cruelty,' he said, 'for mental and physical cruelty. She'd no grounds. No real – no morally justifiable grounds. I'm to be headmaster of Lovell's now. It's one of the finest schools in Scotland . . . I love my work. I'm a first-class schoolmaster. I shouldn't have got Lovell's if I hadn't been. I'm a sane, well-balanced man. Perhaps you don't believe that. Perhaps you think – people who kill must be mad or wicked. I'm neither mad nor wicked. I was a *good* man. But even a good man must have some weakness. Ask yourself: have you no weakness? Greed, sloth, jealousy. The most perfect of us. The Achilles heel is somewhere.'

He was trying to justify himself, she saw, not merely to her but to himself.

'Mine is anger. My judgements of myself are severe: so they are of other people. I can't tolerate the ranker sins. At times I have an awkward temper. It never shows. I control it. I *had* controlled it. But she drove into that weakness. Have you ever had that happen to you? It's like a drill on an exposed nerve. The one nerve that you have learned to govern and protect. My God! if there was cruelty, it was hers, not mine!'

'Everybody says you're a good schoolmaster,' she replied.

For a second there was agreement and pain in his eyes, showing through the fixed intention to kill.

'I know. I have the finest understanding of boys. I can take the dull boy and give him the glow of a new ambition. I can steady the wayward, imaginative child and teach him true concentration; and above all I can give boys a sense of moral values, a thing more than ever vital to them today. But she wanted to snatch it all away, to smash that gift childishly for the vindictive pleasure. And she wasn't merely destroying what I had built, she was depriving hundreds of children, some yet unborn, of what I had to give! It's a thing so *few* have to give. D'you understand? D'you know what I'm talking about?'

She felt that much of what he was claiming for himself was true.

'Yes . . .'

'Did you know that she called herself Elizabeth Talbot?
I never knew her real name until she was dead. She was in
love with your husband. She saw him that night. D'you
know she still believed he would come back to her? She
told me so. I told her not to be a fool, but she said he
would get tired of you and come back to her. It was a
mania with her. D'you know why she married me? Because I reminded her of him. That's all. She told me that
that last night too. I knew something was wrong almost
from the start of our marriage; but what chance had I
against a myth of her own creating? D'you think I care
if he swings? D'you think I care?'

The old restraints were slipping, and the added censors
of these last six weeks. He checked himself and glanced
at the deaf man.

'Yes. I think you care,' she said.

He smiled. 'Then you're wrong. Utterly, damnably
wrong. He's ruined my life—'

'It wasn't his fault.'

'No,' he said viciously, 'it's never their fault, the play-
boys and the pleasure-seekers. They just follow their own
impulses and other people be hanged! What would
Talbot care that he broke up my life. Why should I care
if the consequences come back on him!'

She said: 'Why didn't you let her divorce you?'

'Because it would have finished me. Divorce for cruelty
would have finished my career. And she meant to finish
me. Nothing else would satisfy her. She told me that.
She'd got proof: she'd been to the doctor with some
trifling bruises. Don't you see?'

The train flashed through a station: a porter wheeling
luggage, a pram, two women staring. A level-crossing
and a horse and cart; open country again.

He was looking right through her, his angry uncompromising eyes narrowed and strained.

'Weren't you to blame at all?' she asked.

That brought his gaze back into focus. He half smiled in a contemptuous way.

'My conscience is my own.'

'And God's.'

He took a deep breath. 'Your damned presumption . . .' Her remark was the first somehow truly to touch him. 'D'you think I don't know that? I knew it even on the night.'

'Then how could you kill her?'

'I argued with her, pleaded with her. Yes, *I did*. Not all for my own sake but for hers. All I asked for myself was that the break between us should be done decently. She was amused at that, tormented me with – with my pride – my pride as a scholar, as a schoolmaster, my *justifiable* pride. In spite of everything else she might have been alive but for that . . .'

He was breathing quickly now. '. . . But for that . . .'

There was silence for some time. She knew she had done something, fended him off, that she had somehow shaken him if only for a second; but she did not know how to go on. She hadn't the insight, the knowledge of him.

Oh, God, she thought, show me what to say next.

The deaf man had been rustling his paper, but she did not dare to take her eyes off Fleming.

. . . Suddenly she was conscious that the deaf man was standing up. She turned her head to see him leaving the carriage.

'Don't go! Don't go!'

But his back was to her. She was too late.

As she jumped to her feet Fleming hit her between the eyes. . . .

She fell back upon her seat, the carriage swinging dizzy and sick.

Fleming was fumbling with the carriage door. There was nothing to stop him now. But the train was rushing through a small town: not here; it couldn't be done here. He got up quickly and, still watching her, pulled down the blinds on the corridor side.

'What you do to me,' Philippa got out desperately, 'won't help you now.'

He did not speak but pulled down the last blind.

'I found a photograph of your wife,' she said.

He watched her in sudden alarm. 'You're lying . . .'

'On the school photograph,' she whispered. 'I bought a print.'

That had struck him just like a physical blow in return. He saw the truth, that it was true. His eyes went to the suitcase.

'I've posted it,' she said, 'to Scotland Yard.'

The train rushed out into the open country again, but he did not stir, standing by the corridor door. She suddenly realized that his breath was coming as quickly as hers.

He moved to her suitcase, pulled it from the rack.

He tore open the lid, began groping through it, paused to wipe the sweat out of his eyes, groped again, emptied the things out on the seat.

He stopped. '*Where* is it?'

He was like a man gone mad.

'*Where is it?*'

'I posted it as soon as I bought it this morning, the man's name was Baird, he charged half a crown. I marked the photo and posted it at the next stop but one, that was why I missed the first train.' She hardly knew what she was saying.

He stared at her as if he could tear her to pieces. Her bag was behind her, out of sight. She fought the fear out of her eyes and stared back at him.

Suddenly he sat down heavily opposite her. 'You're lying!' he said again. 'Oh God . . . Oh, God . . .'

She leaned back upon her bag and watched him. He made no move. Twenty minutes, she thought. I've got to fight for at least twenty minutes more. Help me. Help me.

The stoker said, looking at the disappearing Selby: 'That's where I was born and that's where me home is. I pass it dozens of times a year, but all I ever see of it is the blasted chimneys.'

The engine driver looked at the pressure gauge and thought: You wonder sometimes, coh, you wonder sometimes, why did I ever get married, and then you think, better that than to be a thin shrivelled little grouser like Bob. He blew the whistle. They were two minutes late, and this head wind . . .

The deaf man said: 'Pardon me, are they serving tea yet?' and screwed in his ear-piece.

'Yes,' said the woman standing in front of him. 'But the tables are all full. We'll have to wait a few minutes.'

Philippa said as Fleming raised his head: 'What difference does it make? You can't escape from what you did.'

His face was old and tired. 'I had until you came.'

'You killed Elizabeth because she drove you to it. Isn't that what you said?'

'Yes.'

'In great anger?'

'Well?'

'But now you were going to kill me – in cold blood?'

'I can do it just the same.'

'But not in anger. Not with excuse. All these weeks haven't you been thinking: "I had excuse. She drove me to it. She was wicked. I could do no other." *Haven't* you?'

He looked at her, frowning, puzzled at her perception, yet his reason answering hers.

'It's the truth!'

'But you'll never be able to say that about me.' She straightened up, no longer so much on the defensive. 'Don't you *see*? When you kill it doesn't solve anything, it just begins all over again. You can never get away from it. Never! Evil brings evil, for ever and ever, without end.'

He turned sharply in his seat, and she thought she had gone too far. But his gaze travelled past her to the hurrying countryside and the rain.

'You're a Christian, aren't you?' she said.

He muttered: 'For you to talk of Christianity to *me*, who've practised it as you've never begun to think of doing! . . .'

'You're a man of principles,' she went on. 'Religion means a lot to you, doesn't it? You believe death doesn't end everything. Don't you?'

'Be quiet!' he said, facing the devils in his own soul, all those devils of torment and doubt which for six weeks had been rigidly under his mind's control.

'A religious man without the courage of his beliefs.' She was attacking now.

He shook his head, as if to shake away her words. For a long time there was silence. In this his logical mind could no longer help him, for she was attacking him through it.

But when he looked at her again she knew she could not let up.

'And those boys,' she said quickly, 'at Penmair. Teaching them has been the real love of your life. You've told me so. Can you guide them with this on your conscience? *Can* you? If your mind is twisted it will give a twist to theirs. A moral warp like a – an ugly deformity! Did you ever believe you could take up your work at Lovell's with this thing between you and them?'

A goods train screamed past them on its way north.

When the vibration and the noise were past, slowly, very slowly, he said: 'I'll make a bargain with you.'

All the weakness and faintness in her cried out, 'Yes, yes, what is it?' but instead she said:

'You've nothing to bargain with.'

Slowly again he said: 'Give me a chance. Your precious Talbot is safe. Give me a few hours.'

With a queer twisted compassion moving in her she said:

'Your chance has gone. Don't you see that? You do. In your heart you've always known it. Nothing I can do can change it. Nothing you can do to me can change it. You loved Elizabeth, didn't you?'

'I hated her!'

'You loved Elizabeth, and your life finished when you killed her. Nothing can be the same again. By killing her you defeated yourself. It isn't a chance to save your life you need now, it's a chance to save your soul. . . .'

There was another silence.

Suddenly he sprang to his feet and wrenched at the door. At first she shrank back, mistaking his intention. But then as the door swung open she caught at his arm.

The pressure of wind and her hold frustrated that first impulse. He struggled and cried out and loosed his hold of the door to strike at her. He hit her arm viciously above the elbow, but she caught with one hand as pain opened the other.

He was dragging her with him, himself half out, when suddenly another form came upon them from behind, clutching at them both, pulling them to safety.

Half fainting, with shouts and questions in her ears, she saw Fleming fall back upon the seat opposite her. Sweat was running down his face, and defeat seemed to be in the depths of his heart.

The deaf man had come back in time.

Chapter Twenty-six

THE JUDGE HAD begun his summing-up at a quarter to
three and had finished it at twenty to four. Tyler, Nick
knew, had been annoyed at certain opinions the judge had
expressed, and in so far as anything to displease Tyler was
bad for Nick, the summing-up might be considered
slightly adverse.

Since then the jury had been out and so far showed no
sign of returning. Nick was in the prisoners' room and it
was now well after five.

The prison doctor had called once, but soon went away
satisfied that he was standing up to the strain. Then
shortly after, Archer had come. He had stood there and
asked the warder a few routine questions, looking faintly
ill at ease; had exchanged a dozen sentences with Nick
and had gone out. It was queer, Nick thought, they hadn't
liked each other at first; apart from the ordinary obvious
antagonism coming from the fact that Archer was trying
to pin something on him, there had been that small
personal antagonism always between them, which would
have existed however they had met. But that had gone.

They were still enemies because of their present situation, but the personal dislike was no longer there. Underneath reason, which would not admit it, the instinct of
each recognized honesty in the other.

At a quarter to six a warder came in.

'Not touched your sandwiches, Mr Talbot?'

'No, thanks.'

'They're tasty enough. Bit of ham. Not too fat. Do you
good.'

Nick smiled slightly, since it seemed only kind to humour the man who was trying to humour him.

'I brought your cigarettes.'

'Thanks.' Nick accepted the packet but did not at once open it. 'Any sign of a move yet?'

'Not yet, sir.'

'It's a bit unusual, isn't it, being so long?'

'Oh, lord, no. They're like this sometimes. You remember that case of the fire-watcher: did his wife in. They were three hours and twenty minutes over that.'

Nick got up. 'Any news of my wife yet?'

'Not so far as I know, sir.'

'What time are the trains from Edinburgh, d'you know?'

' 'Fraid I don't.' The warder piled up the tray. 'Sure you won't have a bite?'

'Er – no, thanks.'

The warder got as far as the door with the tray when he paused. He had caught the sound of feet coming down the corridor. He drew back as the door opened and another warder appeared. He glanced at Nick.

'Well?'

The newcomer glanced at the warder with the tray.

'Just moving now, Bill.'

Nick felt his stomach go cold. He bent and opened the packet of cigarettes and took one out.

'Have I time for this?'

'Well, just a few puffs, sir.'

Nick was grateful that the warder held a lighter to the end of the cigarette. It would have been humiliating if his own hands hadn't been steady.

He drew at the cigarette, feeling the smoke fill his lungs. He drew at it again. The warder had set down the tray and was waiting for him.

After a few moments Nick bent and screwed out the end in the ash-tray.

'Now,' he said.

The six-forty-one Edinburgh–King's Cross was on time. The powerful locomotive steamed into the station, and as the train slowed to a stop doors opened all along its length like gills breathing on some strange elongated submarine fish.

People poured out of it, porters caught up luggage, men on motor trolleys shouted, the mass congealed, spread across the platform, began to escape past the engine to the taxis and the street.

Out of a first-class carriage came the deaf man. He had had the most harassed and difficult journey of his life. Following him came Philippa and Sidney Fleming. There was a dark bruise on Philippa's forehead; Fleming was deadly pale like a man who had just been sick.

The deaf man said: 'Don't you think . . . Wouldn't it be better . . .'

She shook her head at him. 'Thank you, no.'

'The police . . .'

'No, no . . .'

Fleming was moving on, and she took hurried steps to catch up with him. But not quite to catch up. She walked at his elbow. The deaf man watched them go.

They reached the barrier and passed through, walked out of the station.

The journey had been a nightmare, intolerable with the strain of waiting: a taut wire that must soon snap. The deaf man had wanted to stop the train; all through it she had had her way with both of them. Something beyond herself, stronger than herself. Fleming had sat in a queer half-stupor, chin sunk, staring at the floor. Every time he stirred or sighed or cleared his throat she had expected a new move, a recovery, a crouching to attack. The stop at Doncaster had been the worst time of all.

A woman had come along and stared in at the carriage, and then, perhaps put off by something almost waxwork in the attitude of the people within, had moved away again. But her presence, peering in if only for a moment, had roused Fleming, and he stretched out a hand as if to open the door. Then he abruptly sat back and his gloved hands dropped on his lap. For a time after the train restarted he sat with eyes closed, breathing heavily as if there was no air. Once she began to wonder if he had had a stroke. But later he had come round, and in a moment when her attention had strayed, she had glanced back at him and found his eyes fixed on her. But something in the gaze again lacked personal focus.

Now at last they were in London. She was still in danger but would have her way; she still carried the photo in her handbag; if he recovered now . . .

To snatch the bag and open it was easy, to escape, to thrust her away and take to his heels. There was only the invisible tie of her understanding. That understanding was also a challenge – to his integrity, to his beliefs. She'd no control over him but the greatest control of all.

There was a policeman standing by the station entrance. Fleming moved towards him. She put a hand on Fleming's arm, but he shook it off.

'Where is the nearest police station?' he said.

The constable glanced at him curiously, at his intent, scholarly, deathly face.

'Down Flower Street, sir. Second on your left.'

'Thank you.' Fleming moved off again.

It was raining hard, a straight steady downpour, and the blobs of water made erratic patterns in the pools. The tyres of the buses hissed and splashed mud across the road. The rush hour was over, but there were plenty of people about.

He waited patiently at a crossing like the other people going home to their villas and their little warm suburban houses. He crossed and turned left and they came to Flower Street. Now, she thought, a hundred yards more.

He went down it, with rain falling on his face, and as they drew nearer to the small police station – which seemed so unobtrusive among the business offices and the shops – she drew a pace closer, watching him with the last remains of her stamina. If there was a bond between them – a bond, a challenge, an ascendancy and a failure – then never must it be surer than now. Every normal instinct would fight to break it.

At the very foot of the steps he hesitated and turned. Their eyes – which had met so often today in a conflict of wills – met for the last time. It was as if at this last moment the reality of what he had to do was suddenly clear to him in all its sordid and dismal reality. The ordinary man and the fanatic were there together. Self-preservation and self-redemption.

He licked his lips but did not speak.

A policeman came down the steps and passed them close.

Fleming said: 'Good-bye, Mrs Talbot.'

She tried to speak but at first could not, and when she found her voice his back was to her mounting the steps.

He hesitated on the threshold and then passed inside. . . .

Somehow she never doubted his actions now. There was no subterfuge or trick. In any case she hadn't the strength or the relentlessness to climb the steps and see.

She walked on a dozen yards and then all the street

squeezed into a narrow blur of nausea and she staggered and almost fell. She found a low wall and put her face in her hands.

Gone Lovell's, gone Penmair, gone Fleming. I was a *good* man. I can take a dull boy and give him the glow of a new ambition. Moral values. All things were strong and rigid in him. To the last unbending. That was why Elizabeth had gone, why she had not. Good and evil, born in one man, grown in one man, ruined together. . . .

'All right, dearie?' said an old woman passing by.

She nodded and got up. The photo. That too had defeated him. She must take it. At once. At once.

A taxi. There were no taxis here. She turned back immediately towards the main road. Get to Nick. The trial must be stopped.

Perhaps from Flower Street police station they were already telephoning. Or would they take him for a harmless crank? Ask yourself: have you no weakness? he had said. The Achilles heel is somewhere. Mine is anger. Mine is anger.

She reached the end of the street, but could not see a vacant taxi and the buses ground past unheeding. Instead she saw a newsboy on the opposite side of the street. The posters were up.

'*Trial Verdict.*' '*Talbot Trial Verdict.*'

Oh, God, so I've failed!

She walked across the road, splashing and splashed by buses dangerously near. She fumbled in her bag, found a shilling, took the paper.

Her hands trembled so much that the wet paper tore. Then she saw it in the stop-press. 'Jury after two hours' retirement, found Nicolas James Talbot not guilty of murder of Elizabeth Rusman at Old Bailey today.'

She dropped the paper in the mud and found some

pennies change in her hand and walked off down the street.

So it's all been useless, she thought: my effort, my forty-eight hours of striving, of danger. And Fleming's confession. Fleming's life. She was a fool . . . crying for the moon. She loved your husband. What chance had I against a myth of her own creating?

British justice. A triumph. A triumph for justice. Or was it a triumph for Tyler? Oh, Nick . . .

She began to cry, weakly, and had to stop against a wall.

She turned her back to the street and leaned against the wall, staring at the blitzed building and the rubble. No one noticed. The tears ran down her cheeks helplessly. Oh, Nick! So he was free anyhow. The benefit of the doubt. She was crying from fatigue and relief and relaxed nerves. Nick was free. And she was free. Would she sing again? Could she sing again? What would Ravogli say? Would he welcome her? Would people welcome her after all this? Could she sing? . . .

Nick was free. Free already. Yes, she could sing. She fumbled in her bag, fingered the rolled photo, found a bit of a handkerchief and wiped her eyes. She moved away from the wall and began to walk. She didn't know where she was walking, except that it was in the direction of the Old Bailey.

It was still raining and her shoes and stockings were soaked. Nick was free. *The benefit of the doubt.*

And suddenly she saw that all her efforts had *not* been in vain. For the prestige of the police was so high that ever after people would think that Nick had in fact only been given the benefit of the doubt. In law not guilty, but in fact not proven. Free as the next man, but left with a stigma which would cling and cling.

Not that now. This photograph, Fleming's confession,

would change all of it. Nick would be truly and completely mind and heart free. 'Next week-end we'll go down to Joan's together. From then on we'll really start everything over afresh.' Well, they could now. Starting afresh. Nothing in their way. The nightmare was over.

Unconsciously her walk had quickened. Her sight was still blurred, and rain and tears made a sort of kaleidoscope of the moving traffic. People pushed against her, but she kept on her way.

She knew she would keep on her way now until she found Nick, and then they would go on their way together.

Down the long, shining distorted vista of the wet street she walked, heedlessly, tearfully, happily; through the pouring rain.